Over His Rainbow

Over His Rainbow

A Single Woman's Journey to God's Promise

Kathy O'Keefe

To order additional copies of this book, contact:
Xlibris Corporation
1-888-795-4274
www.Xlibris.com
Orders@Xlibris.com
83167

Contents

DEDICATION

This is to all of those, young and old, to help them be who God has called them to be.

This is for all of those, young and old, to reveal the scars of poor decisions.

But most of all it's for all of those who feel they are not worthy of forgiveness and love.

And last but not least, this is for the loves of my life: my family and friends, who, like Christ, helped me up each time I fell.

Acknowledgements: Pastors: Tom Martin, Scott Mooberry, David Emmons at Grace Bible Church, Newfane NY. Pastor Jerry Gillis The Chapel at Crosspoint, Amherst NY, Pastor Stephen Hay at First Baptist Church of Wilson NY. Cover artwork by Pastor Stephen Hay.

Cover art work by Pastor Stephen Hay.

Preface

This book started as a personal account of my journey of faith. What it revealed was the ache of my heart for all who love, for all who long to be loved and for all who have loved and lost. It's a journey that reveals sin that was, sin that is, and God's promise of what will be for all who believe and obey. It sets out to explore all the heart issues of sin and how temptation is always luring us to walk away from God's plan for our life. What is exposed is the rawness of the pain that breaks us and the patience, mercy and love that Christ washes over us to heal and transform us.

My hope is that through my experiences and truths that you will find strength in a God who saves even someone like me. My journey has at times been heartbreaking, revealing, quiet and still, and joyous and fulfilling. Step by step I have learned that the idol of my heart, love, has the spirit of a demon, tempting me, back to emptiness and darkness, no matter how far Christ takes me. Even now I need to be resolute in what Christ has taught me and look for guidance in all things—especially those issues of my heart. I am, like all people, a creature of habit, but I believe that God can change that habit; through the work of the Holy Spirit into something that is so uncomfortable, unsatisfying, and distasteful that you can no longer accept it.

For so many single Christian adults it's hard to find fellowship and support in an area that is still taboo talk about. Most Christian ministries are designed around the support of the family unit. However, when that family unit comes apart, the issues that Christians singles struggle with on top of raising the family are at the heart of Christ. Readers will benefit from this book by utilizing it as a tool to teach purity to Christian singles through the use of the Love Promise. It will inspire them to begin their own journey to a Christ-like life and it will give married people a glimpse into the lives of singles and move them to stand with them and enable them to offer support as Christ spoke of supporting the orphaned and widowed.

My testimony is woven into scripture and provides an insight into the spiritual warfare that goes on within the heart when battling lust in today's world. It shows God's mercy and work in every thread of truth that is exposed, and connects the reader with worship music that ties each moment to the passionate relationship we need to have with Christ. It shows the transforming power of Christ in our life through my battles with the Love Idol of my heart. So from my heart to yours: God's Promise! Kathy O'Keefe

The Beginning of My Journey

Throughout my life, my faith was like the wind—strong and forceful at times and silent and still at others—but there remained a constant wispy thread of hope. Growing up through the sixties revolution and unaware of the changes in the world that where going on around me, I always seemed lost even though my whole world was contained within a one mile radius. I walked to school, hung out at Paterson Country Store and Wilson's Pizza Shop, built forts, raced my bike at Nine Hills and played every sport I could. I had a great childhood with two loving, supportive parents: a mother who stayed at home most of our childhood and a father who worked long hours and went school at night to provide us with a comfortable life. For me, though, there was always something lacking: a real connection to God. So I began my journey at a Lutheran Church which was just a stone's throw from my house.

The funny thing was that even in the confines of my small world, I had an extreme imagination. I seemed to get lost in my daydreaming, never focusing on one dream at a time. I would jump from accepting an Academy Award to a Gold medal in the Olympics to winning a big political race. I always felt like Dorothy in the Wizard of Oz, not sure what I wanted but always believing that whatever it was, I wasn't going to find it in my own backyard! I also had a weird feeling that my life would be fleeting, and that there was some greater purpose to my time here. My thirst for fulfillment never seemed to be quenched by external comforts; they didn't hold any real value for me. What I really starved for was attention, not from one person but from everyone.

As my life unfolded, my lack of direction led me down one wrong path to another, from getting pregnant out of wedlock at the age of eighteen, to finding myself married to an alcoholic—I'll call him Glory Days Guy, just like the Bruce Springsteen song. I was caught in a relationship filled with abuse and adultery; with my choices ripped away from me. I thought my dreams were over. My life was not the family portrait I had dreamed of, rather, it was more like a stolen portrait that had been painted over to hide the real masterpiece.

The odd thing about abuse is that the external bruises don't cut as deeply as the internal images do—the look of intimidation that quickly turned to hatred and rage in his eyes, the words that branded me like a scarlet letter sewn to my soul, the picture of him lying in bed with the babysitter—those are the betrayals that stay in my heart. I remember that when I moved home with my daughter after walking in on him, my dad said, "You know he is going to blame this on you." How true his words were. All it took one word of gossip from a jealous so-called friend and I suddenly became the cheater and worse the target of all his anger, which left me battered and pregnant once again. My struggles continued to mount and the pain of my decisions over the next two years created a cycle of fear, self-hatred, and numbness that was cleverly masked by my own strength and will power, and yet through it all, I held tight to my idol.

My idol was love: to be loved, and to safely give love. I never felt worthy of love. I knew logically that my parents loved me, and later, that my children loved me, but the seed of rejection that Satan planted in my heart took root and grew through the years like poison ivy. The leaves of deceit and distrust, watered regularly by gossip and condemnation, grew full on endless vine of broken relationships. I was always riding a merry-go-round of up again, down again relationships. I went from Jack of all Trades Guy, the guy who never held down a steady job, to Politically Correct Guy, who was always trying paint the perfect family portrait, and NFL Cowboy Artist Guy, who was the last of the Desperados. Each of these guys had something to love about them; there seemed to be beauty even in their torment and neediness. But it was the torment that left me feeling as if the only one I could depend on for certain was me, and while Satan silently mocked my pain, repeatedly filling my head with doubt of God's love for a sinner like me, God called me gently and repeatedly to his own.

When I left my first marriage, I left with nothing. I struggled for thirteen years as a single mom and put myself through college, working several jobs at times to make ends meet. I then went on to build an equestrian business that I had dreamed of my whole life. I thought I had finally built my strength and confidence back up again but it all changed when I married once more. After five years of a manic marriage-go-round, my hopes for a long enduring love ended and I struggled once again to untie the knot, leaving my life frayed and my heart hardened. I started to look in the rearview mirror of life, asking God why this keeps happening to me. This started a journey that led me once and for all through my past so that I could have a Christ-centered future.

Years before, I had suffered a broken neck in a car accident and I watched helplessly as my world fell apart. I struggled through my surgeries, and in my mind, lost everything. The right side of my face had slight paralyses, and my hair, which had hung in ringlets all the way down my back, was cut off. Because I was provisional at social services, I could not get paid for my leave so I lost my home, missed my final semester of college and wasn't sure how I would get back to finish. The one saving grace was that I had my mother to help me, because I couldn't even walk to the bathroom. I thought my life was lost and I felt completely broken. I remember one night that I had managed to get to the bathroom, I stood there looking at what barely resembled me, and I just wanted to die. Satan just started a mantra in my head, your kids would be better off with their father. You could never take care of them like this. Who would ever want to be with someone who looked like a cross between Clint Malarchuk; and the elephant man? I had a gash on my throat, my face was disfigured and my head all swollen from a pin; Satan's words spun again and again through my head. I stood there so tempted in that moment to take a fistful of my pain pills and just be done with it. But I just prayed: God help me. Just then, my daughter knocked on the door. I think she asked if I was okay, but all I heard was, "Mom, I need you."

After my recovery I returned to finish my bachelor's degree and went back to work at a job referred to me by my music industry professor. I'll never forget this professor. He looked at me hiding behind my glasses, frumpy skirts and sweaters, hair pulled tightly back, and asked, what someone dressed like Lilith from Cheers was doing in a music industry class. I looked at him and replied, "I want to organize events, and part of that is entertainment." He looked smugly at me, studying me, and said, "Events like weddings?" I was getting miffed, but answered calmly, "No, I would like to develop big events or concerts that would attract people from all over." He grinned at me and asked, how I planned to do that and make money at it. I answered, "I'm not sure, yet, but I've done fundraisers, and I think there is a market for it." He replied, "Maybe you should think about marketing yourself. It's hard to see you as a music promoter." I answered back, "It's hard to see you as music industry professor, but here you are, in your suit and tie." He turned to the class and said, "Class assignment: you will attend the 97 Rock anniversary party at Sinbads, and you will report on your observations of the overall event." He turned to me and said, "I hope you'll show me what a promoter looks like." With that I grinned, because I love to be challenged.

I soon learned was that my professor started out as a drummer in a band, worked for Harvey and Corky—one of the most recognized promotional companies in Buffalo—then went on to work for Citadel Communications for none other than 97Rock. It was good that I didn't know I was in over my head, because I would have never come out of hiding on my own. That night, I left behind the modest me, leftover from my engagement to Politically Correct Guy, and walked into the bar like I owned it in my leather suit and red spiked pumps. I spent the evening in the VIP section surrounded by Kim Mitchell,

Phil Lewis, Gowan, and Lou Gramm, all the while glancing at my professor with a "gotcha" grin.

After that night he truly taught me everything he could, introducing me to the world of music, recording studios, radio stations, record promoters, and getting me a job at Buffalo's top entertainment agency as marketing coordinator for bars and bands, learning the ropes from the best. It didn't take long for me to become "Buffalo's Entertainment Diva," full leather and all. I found myself working in a world of money, sex, and excess, hanging out with national bands, football players, and hockey players. It was an exciting time in Buffalo with Jim Kelly at the helm of the Bills, and Rob Ray duking it out for the Sabres—it was one big party. I would be hanging out with my friend DJ Anthony, and Andre Reed and there would be a long line of young women waiting to see Andre; it was so funny to me. One day Andre called my parents' house looking for me and my son just about had a stroke—that's when I realize that I wasn't in Kansas anymore. On the outside it was a dream job, especially for a girl raised in the middle of nowhere, but my heart just wasn't in it. It would have been easy to fall into a world that seemed to offer so much materially, but really had nothing at all to offer when you looked around at the sin that called your soul. I learned that for me greed masked by corporate good wasn't what I wanted to be a part of. I needed to find substance in my life and as glamorous as the entertainment and corporate world appears, it is very shallow and can leave you feeling empty and used.

Looking back now I know that God was also with me throughout my time in Buffalo because I had hopelessly fallen in love with a club owner who was a self-made man; he was hard-working, respectful, and smart enough to put business before partying. He taught me the art of being the life of the party without risking my life. He was my Miss the Boat Guy. Although my preoccupation with Miss the Boat Guy kept me out of a lot of trouble, he was never in love with me, which made me love him even more and also made me move an hour away from him. He was my drug of choice and I had to quit cold turkey, so I ran to hide at the complete opposite end of Western New York. He was firmly planted on the sandy beaches of Lake Erie, so I staked my claim on the rocky banks of Lake Ontario. I'll never forget the moment I knew it was finally over. He had helped me move into my new farm house in two feet of snow, he picked up the new puppies for my kids, and when it was time to say goodbye, all I could hear in my head was Bonnie Raitt's, "I Can't Make You Love Me."

Once again I was on my own. I had finally received the settlement from my car accident, and I was now living on my dream horse farm in small peaceful harbor town called Wilson. It was funny when I started dating NFL Cowboy Artist Guy. I had run away to the country to hide and there he was, bigger than life, in the middle of my sanctuary. He was so enticing: 6'6, 300 pounds of all man, outside my house playing catch with my son who was lucky to be five feet at the time. My son caught the football and started running at him and my desperado stuck his arm out and wrapped my son around it like a ragdoll. That night he sang karaoke with my parents, and he was so talented—music, art, he was amazing—everything he touched turned to bronze. But he was first and foremost a Cowboy so he was always coming and going. So I focused on settling into the farm. I kept myself busy with maintaining the farm; I became skilled at stacking hay, spreading manure, and fixing fencing as I worked to find joy in my new-found solitude.

Physically, the farm helped build me back up again but mentally, I was suffering from post-traumatic stress and found myself lost in a feeling of loneliness and depression, which brought me to a my knees one spring night. Standing on the hill overlooking the pastures and the creek, surrounded by fireflies, I remember kneeling in tears, arms wide open, asking God to show me what He wanted me to do here—what was the purpose of my being all the way out here? Because if there wasn't a purpose, I was leaving; I couldn't hide out here anymore. The next day a woman approached me about starting a therapeutic riding center at my farm. It was the answer I thought I was looking for—combining my love of horses with my love of children was an awesome idea. I had always been a very outgoing, social person and even though I no longer wanted to live my life on display, I was starving for attention once again. So my answer was a fundraiser! We would do a jamboree on the farm to raise funds for the therapeutic riding center and kick off the opening. You will soon realize that fundraising is my answer to everything, some people eat, I fundraise.

Just before the opening, a woman called about the ribbon cutting for the horseback riding center and we instantly connected; we ended up talking about angels and how she wanted me to meet her son. When I hung up I thought it was odd but the following Saturday by coincidence I met her son (Manic Guy) and he swept me off my feet. This was my prince charming: a sweet, talented man with a lonely, distant son, who had lost his mother and two sisters in a car accident two years earlier. I'll never forget looking into the big blue eyes of this lost little boy who was around the same age as my own son; I just fell in love. I had struggled with the guilt of not having a male role model for my own son and Manic Guy went out of his way to do so much with the boys. The boys were like Tom Sawyer and Huck Finn—what one didn't think of the other did. There was four-wheeling across the creek and through the orchards. There was fishing with 22's, then nailing the fish to a tree to attract other animals, and the best, putting skinned squirrel in my freezer with the tails still on, and forgetting to tell me . . . It was a living Mark Twain adventure. Manic Guy did and said everything right, I thought, finally, a man from a good Christian family—this must surely be God's answer to my prayers. It amazed me that this man who had lost so much could go on living much less smile again, and here I was struggling to get over an accident that I had survived. With all that there was, there was still an uneasiness I just couldn't put my finger on that kept pulling at my heart saying "Don't do it." Even though I was feeling pushed and increasingly uneasy, I ignored my intuition. Right up to the very week before the wedding, I was hesitant and I thought we should call it off and wait, but he manipulated me into marrying him by playing on the loss of his first family. I would soon learn that he was very gifted at the art of manipulation. But more importantly, I eventually learned that sympathy and need are not foundations for a marriage.

It wasn't long before the fairytale turned to a nightmare as I watched mental illness steal away the man I thought I loved. What I would then discover is that the man I thought I knew never existed at all. His behavior became more and more bizarre. From drug and alcohol abuse, homosexual pornography, all the way to a DWI on a tractor pulling a manure spreader, that was my guy! The worst of it was his need to drive a wedge between my own children and friends with his manipulation and lies; as he grew more and more out of control, so did my fears. I couldn't believe that this was the same man I had married. How could I not have seen this? I had opened a small coffee shop in the harbor to give Manic Guy something to do, some structure with accountability and the next thing I knew, people began to gossip about my business relationship with the Harbor developer. The developer was the Master of Marketing, the Baron of Branding, the God of all Gods, (in his mind), who by all accounts would be a great catch for any single woman, (the operative word there is single) but for me, I've never been attracted to the arrogant, Rhett Butler type. It's intriguing and challenging, but not attractive. I think that arrogance creates a competitive spirit within me that is often mistaken for chemistry by those who spar with it and especially by those who watch. Gradually, the gossip pushed Manic Guy to the point of verbal and physical abuse to the point that I would lock myself in the spare room at night. Then one night I awoke and Manic Guy was leaning over me and Satan once again stole my soul. All the memories of my first husband flashed back in my mind, right down to the smell of beer on his breath.

So on top of the embarrassment of my husband I was already dealing with at home, I was trying to protect my stepson, put my farm up for sale, juggle a new business that I didn't really want, deal with my son getting arrested after a graduation party, and my daughter moving home with her "fiancée" who had lost his job, just in time to announce they were having a baby. I also had to face the pain of betrayal from people I thought were my friends as they continued to gossip. It was degrading to think that at forty, with all that I had done on my own, people would still try to minimize my work motivation or interaction to something sexual. What people did not know was that I had learned firsthand what it felt like to be cheated on so cheating was never an option for me, but leaving was something I did well.

I remember sitting alone in the living room in tears completely drained from all that was going on, and Manic Guy came in crying, telling me that I had no time for him, that I was his best friend and that my best friend was my son. I just sat there dumb-founded at his insensitivity, that he had truly no ability to be compassionate to me; it was just another opportunity to dramatically make everything about him. It made me sick to even look at him, so it was once again time to distance myself from the chaos as my world fell apart. But this time, the distance between trusting any man for anything in my life and my heart grew as far apart as the East is to the West.

The unraveling continued with the rumors playing on Manic Guy's mind until he reached his crescendo, and as I stared down the barrel of a shotgun I realized I had been here before. Once again I was living in fear and torment in my own home, walking on eggshells, and I had had enough. I quickly asked God to help me as I challenged him to shoot me. I refused to live life as a victim—I would rather be dead. In that moment not only was the relationship over, but more importantly, I was through being a parent instead of a partner; I realized that my need to be needed had become a license for me to just take over and fix everything. This realization made me vow that this was the last time this would come back to haunt me.

I continued to try desperately to get him help and protect both his son and my own family from harm, but what I found shocked me. In New York State's fluff-filled health care system there was nothing that the mental health system could do or would do unless he harmed himself or someone else. Like so many ridiculous civil rights protection laws, we allow an innocent person to be destroyed before a mentally ill person can be saved from him or herself. So Manic Guy spiraled out of control, self-medicating with alcohol and drugs until he was finally hospitalized after making threats to his mother and father. All that time we tried to get him help and what did they do? They released him in one week, and he took off to Florida. Leaving his son with me, he proceeded to run up all the credit he could get, was arrested for theft, and got a woman without a green card pregnant, all in the three months it took finalize our divorce. Three days after our divorce, I received a phone call that he had been in a motorcycle accident and wasn't expected to make it. It was the hardest moment of my life looking into the face this young man, knowing that he had already lost his mother and two sisters in a car accident, and telling him that he and his grandfather would have to go to identify his father. It still breaks my heart, but thankfully, God had mercy and saved his father, I still believe that having a connection with an "imperfect" parent is better than no connection at all. I remember telling him the same thing I told my kids: "We have to love people for who they are, not what we want them to be." Sometimes we tend to focus on all the things people aren't until we are blinded to all the small moments of good that they bring to our lives.

When it was all over, the house was sold and the kids were safe, I was free for the first time in my life. With the intention of never coming back, I packed up my horse trailer loaded my two show horses up and headed to Florida, but I quickly learned that no matter how far I go I can't run from myself and there truly is no place like home. I remember a Rascal Flatts song I played over and over on my two day drive: "I'm Moving On." Little did I know that I had only begun to deal with my ghosts and face all my demons, and I was far from being at peace with myself. After three months of living my mid-life crisis by purchasing my dream Mustang convertible, having a fling with an Argentinean twenty-something polo player, finally learning the difference between a boat and yacht, riding my horses until finally could finally say, "been there done that," and attending events that were beyond even my vivid imagination, opportunity wasn't just knocking—it was kicking in the door. Yet, as glamorous as it was, that lifestyle just wasn't for me either, and I found myself feeling more empty than ever, so I called my son and told him I was buying a place on the lake and I was heading home.

Needless to say, as I arrived home, my self-confidence sunk back to an all-time low. I went through my ritual of numbing my pain. Some people turn to their addictions, and I turn to attention, so it was time to fundraise! I created my own stage with one charity event after another, painting on a false smile, and going out dancing like I was the only one in the room. My heart cried out, "Look at me! Someone see me!" but no one could see, not even me, that what I was so desperate to avoid and what I feared most was time alone to face myself through God's eyes.

This went on until one night when I was devastated by the words of my sister when she questioned my need to be the center of attention all the time: "Even when you're not trying to get attention, it just happens. Don't you get sick of it? What guy would want to be with someone that every guy in the place is ogling?" Her words pierced my heart and once again my self-hatred, which I thought I had buried, burned in me. I never really understood the impact of my actions, and my words on others; I just thought I would play the part everyone expected of me, because it was easier than standing up for the respect that I deserved. It was always so easy to grab everyone's attention, and as hard as I tried to turn it to something positive, I could never find away to do it where I didn't end up feeling empty and sick of being on parade. I was always torn between the person who everyone expected me to be and the person I was in private. There were so many times that I would try to run away from myself, but Satan always worked my insecurities and my abilities together to put me in front of every temptation. Looking back now it was only by God's grace that I managed to not get lured into the addictions that were only one bad decision away.

After a long, quite ride home my sister apologized as she dropped me off, and I shrugged it off, walked into the house and went straight to my room. I was literally feeling sick of me, of my life, of my choices, and in that moment I could no longer hide from myself, or God. I had walked so long with a numb and hardened heart, trying somehow to protect myself from the rage and fear that I had experienced, that my heart broke open like a dam; the force of the pain brought me to my knees once again. I cried out for Him to save me, because I could no longer live like this anymore, chasing after things that left me feeling so empty. I wanted Him to show me what it was He wanted from me, what works I could do to please Him, not to gain love here but to gain His love, to feel His love, a love I could trust in, and a love that would not fail me or condemn me. I knew the "story" of the cross, but as I lay there I heard a different voice call out to me, not one of ridicule or judgment, just a soft "Who do you say I am?" I knew in that moment that I was missing a true connection with Christ Himself. I had no idea who this man was, and why he would give so much, for just one insignificant person like me. That night through my tears I asked God to reveal His Son to me, so that I could grasp His love, and that was when the real journey began.

Letters from Ruth

I had visited Grace Bible Church several times, as I watched my brother, (who is also my partner in a toy store called Little Voice Books and Toys at the time), grow in Christ. I was captivated by the dedication of the congregation and my brother's family when I saw the Passion play at Easter. There was something I took away with me that night, and it was reconfirmed when I walked through the door just before Christmas. I can't even remember what the service was about; all I heard was one passage, Matthew 16:15-16, when Jesus says to Peter, *"But who do you say that I am?"* Simon Peter replied, *"You are the Christ, the Son of the living God."* I knew that this was where God called me to be. I just felt something I had never felt in all my travels from faith to faith. I knew that day that Gods truth was always there waiting for me to come home; it was in the Gospel. So I picked up my Bible and after shaking the dust off, I started to read. I was insistent on starting from the very beginning and working my way through each book. Even when my sister-in-law suggested starting in the New Testament, I was adamant. I didn't realize that God had other plans, and that my journey to Christ would begin in the book of Ruth.

Each time I went to my Bible I would either find it opened to or it would flip to the book of Ruth, which makes no sense when I didn't even know that there was a book of Ruth. Coming from Lutheranism to then Catholicism, I was shocked at first that I'd never even seen this book before. Then I was intrigued that God actually had such a heart for these two widowed women. So I skipped ahead and read. While I thought it was interesting I didn't really get what I should take away from it, so I went back to the "Beginning." As I grew and became part of the Church through the services, and grace group, I found myself skipping around. In Hebrews, Christ showed me that all my sins were forgiven and forgotten through his sacrifice. Every time Satan tried to whisper in my head I would find myself back at Matthew, hearing "Who do you say I am?" At that time Christ called me to be baptized and to meet Him face-to-face in the waters of life. Each time He asked and I followed, I thought, "I could never exceed this moment of revelation," but once again I would find my Bible opened to Ruth, and I would "glean" through it again to see if there were any seeds I had missed. Then, Pastor Tom announced that we would be going through the book of Ruth that summer and I thought, "That's funny," and then I thought, "Well, maybe there is something I am missing." As we went through it, I was drawn closer to the heart of the story, and I reflected on the life and the struggles that Ruth and Naomi went through. Initially, I didn't think that there were similarities in our journeys, but as I grew closer to them, God revealed the depths of my heart to me and there-in lay my truth. God brought back to the surface what thought I had buried long ago. Although I had forgiven myself and others for the wounds, God revealed to me that the scars were still there and only then did He start to truly heal my pain from the inside out. His work not only came forth within me, but it started to change everything around me, beginning with my business. I felt compelled to change the name of our business to Noah's Ark, and God brought all the pieces of a fragmented business plan together, and He brought out the best of my brother and the best of me. Under the motto "Navigating by Faith" we began to grow by his hand.

My journey through Ruth started out superficially on the mere fact that we were women who went through many struggles, and as God worked in me it began to evolve from a simple love story to a story of redemption. It went from simple "Maybe God has a Boaz in store for me" to a complex, "This is what a man of faith looks like?" A man of faith sows fruit, not to glorify himself, but to glorify God. So the works that we do should not come from a place of self-interest, but a place that reaps a larger harvest for God. I believe Pastor Tom said, "We are responsible to God to work humbly for his glory." I also recognized that even though Naomi initially felt bitterness the loss of her husband and sons she did not let it become who she was; she hung by a thread to her faith and God directed her to their kinsman-redeemer. God, even though He did not intervene, had His own sovereign plan for both Ruth and Naomi. In all my life I just couldn't wait for God's timing, for God's plan; I was always trying to skip ahead. I realized that it was time for me to submit to His authority to turn over my "weapons of self-destruction" and learn to trust in Him. His promise to me was to not let me turn left or right, and that He would keep me focused on Him and reveal to me what the Bride of Christ looks like.

So I learned patience. I learned to put my burdens on Him and wait for His answer; not to react but to respond in a way that is Christ—like. As I went on, slowly but surely, my heart started changing into new ways of thinking. I learned to put me aside, and challenge myself to think beyond this moment to how Christ would want me to respond. I now know that my transformation is for His glory and therefore I cannot hide in what is comfortable and safe.

God brought me to Himself, as He did Ruth to show others that feel like they are unlovable, unworthy, unforgivable, unwelcomed, that God's grace is for all who believe in Him.

Ruth, from the non-Jewish tribe of Moab, lost her husband who taught her the truth of the Lord, left her homeland to travel to a new land, Bethlehem, without a man to protect and provide for her or her mother-in-law. She was then scorned as an outcast and unbeliever, maintained her grace and faith through the gossip and innuendo and provided for herself and Naomi through hard work. Ruth did not leave her mother-in-law and run to what was safe and familiar, or run after other men to provide for herself; she followed God's lead, opening the door for Boaz to be the a testimony of God's grace. Boaz did not boast of his riches and he did not condemn those around him. Boaz empowered Ruth by treating her with respect, allowing her to glean from his fields and offering his protection without putting his own self-interest first. Even when Ruth came to the threshing floor in the middle of the night to offer herself to Boaz, he did not give in to selfish desire brought on by drunkenness; he sent her home with his promise to redeem her so that all would know she was a worthy woman. God then showed me a clear picture of what love should look like in 1 Corinthians 13:6-8; *Love is patient and kind: love does not envy or boast; it is not arrogant or rude. It does not insist on its own way; it is not irritable or resentful; it does not rejoice at wrongdoing, but rejoices with the truth. Love bears all things, believes all things, hopes all things, endures all things. Love never ends.*

I was feeling quite at peace with my new revelation when God prodded me further. Pastor Tom announced that we would be doing the Book of Ruth for our Easter outreach, and once again there it was. At this point I was on the line between "Yeah, this is unbelievable," and "Oh no—now what have I done?" So as I revisited my old friends, I asked, "What more can I glean from three pages?" So that night as I read, Ruth 4:17 called to me and God reminded me that I no longer have to go looking for my Kinsman Redeemer, that God sent to me, through Ruth, the Redeemer of all Redeemers. After all this, He led me lovingly back to the cross. I was overwhelmed with the images of Christ on the cross and He wrapped me in His love and gave me a peace that I had never known.

Now you would think my story ends there, but the life of Ruth continued to weigh heavily on my heart. Then by accident I prayed out loud about my experience and my hopes for the ensemble of Ruth. After a week of discomfort He awoke me from my sleep and in tears I knew that my experience was not about me, just as Ruth is not a story about two women; it is their testimony to everyone that God is at work and His plan is sovereign, and we are called to give testimony of His work in us. I reached for my old Bible that I started this journey with and read my notes. There at the bottom, in reference to the

Book of Ruth ending with a new beginning through the birth of Christ, I had at one point written, "My story is not over yet!" and I once again took my pen and added, "It starts today with my testimony." I will share my story no matter the cost so others will learn of how the timeless love story of Ruth leads to the greatest love story of Christ.

I know that I have to trust in God and feel safe in His love for me, letting go of my own will to make things happen, knowing that His plan for me is greater than any dream I may have on my own. I will be strong in Him—not me and not someone else. It is one thing to want someone to lean on in your life; it is another to put that need before leaning on God. Long before I was in existence, my knight in shining armor made the ultimate sacrifice for me. I ask you, "What more can one give to capture your heart then what Christ gave on the cross?" He calls to me a simple request: "Open your heart to me and I will give you eternity," and yet, I fail Him every day. The amazing thing is that now in midst of my failure I can rejoice because, through Christ, I recognize my failure and can rest in His forgiveness. As He continues to unravel every strand of my life, He reveals, heals, and appeals to my heart. It brings me great joy in those moments that the Holy Spirit reaches out to let me know that, "you are mine!"

Letters from Hebrews

While I was repeatedly drawn back to the book Ruth, Pastor Tom was also covering the Book of Hebrews. What better book to argue my need to once and for all commit to Christ? It was in the midst of finding Christ that I met a man who would help to open me up to a whole new realm of spirituality. He was my Charismatic Christian Guy, and I mean that in a completely loving way. Even to this day he brings a smile to my face. He had the heart of Christ and the beauty of King David; his stature was like an image of David as he threw those stones at Goliath. At face value, Charismatic Christian Guy was truly God's work of art. He had the most loving, generous heart; you could picture him as King David worshiping in his underwear. The depth of his love for Christ was like that of an ocean, but like David, he too had great struggles in his walk with the Lord. God showed me through him that even the most faithful fall, but through Christ we can rise again. The book of Hebrews made me face my own sin, but it also taught me the greatness of God's forgiveness through Christ and discernment in the hypocrisy of many religions and myself.

In Hebrews I noticed a reoccurring theme of not falling into unbelief, and I recognized that though I thought I believed in God, I really never fully believed in His love for me or His sacrifice for me. I remembered when I became Catholic and I went through all the rituals of getting confirmed, again, getting an annulment before a tribunal; hoop after hoop I jumped all the way to teaching CCD classes. I felt connected to the history of the church, the idea of being Irish Catholic and a Democrat just like the Kennedys, but beyond that, I felt nothing; I still felt empty. I remember going to confession for the first time, and as I walked away absolved from my sin, I felt numb. All I could hear was, "What God could ever forgive my greatest sin and why would He? Because I couldn't; I wouldn't." Out of pain, anger and hatred for myself, I had convinced myself through worldly acceptance to make a decision that would follow me and haunt me the rest of my life. Even in my time of ignorance, I knew in my heart that worldly views were not Godly views, but I convinced myself while working my college internship at Planned Parenthood that a fetus was just a clump of inconvenient cells that I could not afford to have. So the one time I had the choice, I took control of the situation making the worst decision of my life. I allowed people who disguise themselves as people who care for the future of my life to manipulate me into a self-righteous act that supports their own agenda. Why is it that some people believe that just because a child is unplanned that it will be unwanted? Why is it that they believe it is better to achieve than conceive? Who decided that a woman's right to choose was more important than a child's right to life? This is not an economic issue, this is a heart issue. Who have we become? Who have I become? All of this raced through my head, so instead of feeling forgiven, I somehow felt more condemned, realizing for the first time what I had done. It was like the burden I already carried was even heavier than before, and I became acutely aware of a debt that I could never pay. Shortly after that I made the decision to have my tubes tied; I felt I was undeserving to receive a gift so great.

I never understood why I gradually felt worse than when I began my Catholic journey as time went by. I thought there was something wrong with me that I felt no connection to the Church body and no attachment to the scripture. It was like I was caught in a remake of the Stepford Wives going through the motions of religion. I could never put my finger on it, but something told me it wasn't right and I couldn't live with what I saw as hypocrisy, let alone to accountable to God for teaching it to innocent children. Gradually questions rang out to me like a church bell: where in the Bible does it say to pray for people in purgatory or pray to Mary? Nowhere. And yet that was what was taught. In Luke 11:27, Christ corrected a follower when he had called out, *Blessed is the womb that bore you*, Christ responded, *Blessed rather are those who hear the word of God and keep it!* The same rituals that I thought would draw me closer to God were the same rituals that made me question the road I had chosen. The truth is that my forgiveness and salvation is by faith in Christ alone, but this revelation did not come to me until Christ came alive within me through the Holy Spirit in the book of Hebrews.

I remember so clearly sitting there listening to Pastor Tom say that "sins are not just forgiven but forgotten," and not to punish ourselves for sin, but to trust in what Christ did for us. Christ replaced the legalism of the Old Testament with the final sacrifice. No more rituals, no more works of man, no more prices to be paid—just faith in Christ. Christ bore it all. And as I sat there just trying to wrap my mind around that, he read Hebrews 9:14: *How much more, then will the blood of Christ, who through the eternal Spirit offered himself unblemished to God, cleanse our consciences from acts that lead to death, so that we may serve the living God!* He then asked, "How much more must Christ pay for our sins than what he paid as he was nailed upon that cross?" I just sat there and tears came over me and I could not contain what was in my heart. It was like Christ was standing before me with his hands out to me, asking, "Kathy, what more can I do to convince you that I love you? I know you, you are my creation; you cannot hide from me what I already know. I am not holding you in judgment, but asking you to trust and believe in me, your sacrifice." I just crumbled and as usual, I was unprepared and God provided—my sister-in-law handed a box of Kleenex to me.

From that moment on I was convicted in my heart to do what I could to do to open my heart and mind to Christ and to this day He has not failed me. With that conviction Christ introduced me to the Holy Spirit in Hebrews as well, and through Him I was and am nurtured and disciplined as He plucks the stones from my eyes and my heart. Hebrews 10:14 says: *Because by one sacrifice he has made perfect forever those who are being made holy.* Pastor Tom pointed out that we are actively being made in Christ's image; it is an on-going process of transformation. In Hebrews 10:15 it goes on to say that the Holy Spirit also testifies to us about this: *This is the covenant I will make with them after that time, says the Lord. I will put my laws in their hearts, and I will write them on their minds.* Then it adds: *Their sins and lawless acts I will remember no more. And where these have been forgiven, there is no longer any sacrifice for sin.* For the first time I felt the Holy Spirit and I knew through Hebrews that I, too, could persevere with my new journey.

What I wasn't prepared for was the revelation of my own sin, and how that had played out in my relationships throughout my life. That which was socially acceptable no longer felt comfortable, and each time I would grow, I recognized a time of beginning and a time for ending. The first of these endings was with my Charismatic Christian Guy. It was a slow revelation about my inability to stand for what was acceptable behavior in my life. CCG was the first Christian man I had dated since my marriage; it had been three years, and I found myself following his lead in the word instead of seeking the truth for myself. When it came down to it I chose Christ. I could not be double-minded in my faith. The fruition of the man that I saw over time was not that of a selfless, Christ driven man, but of a man seeking power through the gifts of the Holy Spirit. I was so impressed by the knowledge he had of the scripture that we could talk for hours about what was taught in service. It was exciting and enticing to me; I started to grow in ways I wasn't expecting including the discernment that came with that growth.

I started to question society's belief that there is nothing wrong with having sex out of the context of marriage. For many years I didn't see anything wrong with it, as long as I was in a committed relationship. I didn't have to have a piece of paper to show my commitment. The actual truth was that being divorced twice proved that I didn't need a piece of paper because not even that could bind my heart to someone. I would go from relationship to relationship repeating the same actions expecting a different outcome. Even though time after time it never brought me happiness, I never admitted that the reason could be my own inability to wait for the right man. My relationships were based on nothing more than skin-deep attraction; I felt men were more in love with the idea of being with me than the concept of being in love with who I am. My attraction was based on need, a strong need to feel that someone, anyone, loved me.

That all changed when I turned my failure over to Christ. I would hear a new voice in my head, the Holy Spirit questioning me, "Is this what a man of Christ looks like?" And little by little he revealed the hypocrisy of what was before me. It was funny to hear the scripture used to defend what is simply wrong by Christian standards. It was as if bending in one area led to bending in another area for Charismatic Christian Guy; he could easily rest in God's forgiveness of his intentional sin, or better yet, blame his sin on spiritual warfare, which to some extent I now know is true. I also saw a conflict with the teaching of his church that just tugged at my heart, I knew that it was just not right, and when I questioned it, he felt that I was questioning his authority. The more I questioned his walk, from financial irresponsibility to even our sexual intimacy, the more his anger grew. This led to drunkenness, which led to drug use. For the first time in my life, I had someone standing before me yelling at me in tongues; strange, but after all, we are talking about my life. In Hebrews 13:8 it says: *We are warned not to be carried away by all kinds of strange teachings*, so I began to pray for wisdom in this time of learning, because I knew I could not match his scripture knowledge with my own.

I kept going back to Hebrews 10:26: *If we deliberately keep on sinning after we have received the knowledge of the truth, no sacrifice for sin is left*. Hebrews is packed with warnings against unbelief and falling away so I knew that I needed to base my perceptions on the truth of the scripture not on emotional need. So I went to Acts 2, 1-13 which discusses the birth of the Holy Spirit through tongues, allowing the disciples to minister in the language of other nations, and then I went to Acts 10:44 in which the Holy Spirit spreads God's message through the speaking of tongues; much like God divided the nations at Babel, now He would unify them through tongues. After finding God's purpose for the gift of tongues, I found myself in 1 Corinthians 12-14, and that is where I rested in God's wisdom, because it was here that God's will for the use of tongues is revealed. The two things that Paul stresses are that "sensational" gifts must not be elevated above sound instruction and that the gifts should only be used in orderly and proper worship not confusion. When I attended CCG's church it was overwhelming, people speaking in tongues, dancing around with flags, and laying on the floor, you could definitely feel something, and it was emotional, but the teaching was lost in the drama. In 1 Corinthians

14:19, Paul says, *But in the church I would rather speak five intelligible words to instruct others than ten thousand words in a tongue.* He goes on in 14:22 to say, *Tongues, then are a sign, not for believers but for unbelievers; prophecy, however, is for believers, not for unbelievers.* Throughout it all, Paul stresses that all gifts be used to edify God with love.

I really needed God's wisdom to understand all of this because in one breath Paul is saying not to forbid speaking in tongues and be eager to prophesy, and yet our Church doesn't believe in this doctrine. Then in the same breath he says women should remain silent in the churches. They are not allowed to speak, but must be in submission, and if they have a question they should inquire of their husbands. The Church upholds that doctrine. There must not have been any single women who attended Church then, because not having a husband myself, I had to put all my faith in Him who truly loves me and wait on His answers. After reading through a litany of those who by faith followed God's calling and suffered torture and persecution but moved forward towards God's plan at all cost, never even seeing God's promise for themselves, I realized that that if I wanted that unshakable faith, I had to obey what the Holy Spirit had written on my heart.

I remember what Charismatic Christian Guy told me when we broke up: "You have loved to find that you are a fighter and I have fought to find I am a lover." That stayed with me for the longest time until Christ showed me that my strength is built on Him and He is my warrior. It is easier to dismiss the truth with a romantic statement than accept discipline, and as much as God loves, He will discipline just as much. In Hebrews 12:11 it says; *No discipline seems pleasant at the time, but painful. Later on however, it produces a harvest of righteousness and peace for those who have been trained by it.* So, for this season I am staying focused on Christ and reminding myself daily that, as it says in Hebrews 12:4; *In my struggle against sin, I have not yet resisted to the point of shedding my blood.* Like all of my relationships I try to find the beauty in the ashes and Charismatic Christian Guy showed me how God responds to prayer from my heart rather from ritual. Charismatic Christian Guy helped me turn over to Christ a horrifying nightmare that had repeatedly haunted me for decades: I would wake at approximately the same time of night to a man leaning over my bed, and I would be in such fear I would scream and strike out at him; I thought I was going to have a stroke. I prayed together with Charismatic Christian Guy for Christ to bind this spirit and cast it under His feet, and to this day I have not experienced that dream again. I also took with me Charismatic Christian Guy's gift of worshipping with all your heart as I continued my journey, and I now know that it is through Christ alone, by faith alone, that I am not alone.

P.S. I also took away a great love for Christian music, my favorite, including every Casting Crowns CD, and the song, "I Will Walk by Faith" by Jeremy Camp:

> Well, I will walk by faith, even when I cannot see,
> Well because this broken road prepares Your will for me.

It reminds me that my life is no longer about me but about Christ, and that I put my faith in Him and His plan for my life, no matter how hard it is.

Letters from James

I have often heard of God referred to as the potter who gently and carefully shapes our character, but I am also aware that there are times when the potter mashes the clay and starts over. Those are the times that brought me to book of James. My journey of transformation has been filled with great joy and humbling heartache, but I pray that he will continue to bring the pieces of my life together to create a picture of himself, even though I am often puzzled as to why he would even call my name, considering I am such a creature of habit. About a year and half after Charismatic Christian Guy I started dating a guy who had began to attend Grace with me. He found that he was called to the book of James; his life was in turmoil at that time. Things seemed to be coming up against him in every area of his life and it was as if he was being tossed like a wave in an endless sea. I believe that this was the motivator for his move from the Catholic Church to Grace. It was difficult going through all the changes God was working in me and watching another person who I had started to love go through such difficult times. I could see Satan struggling so hard to keep him bound to his past and yet I also saw God working just as hard. It seemed to be a constant struggle between ego, pride and the perception that he was the "victim guy." Victim Guy believed that everyone is deceptively working to hurt him, betray him, take from him, lie to him, and that he was not responsible for anything that happened to him. God showed me that this is actually a heart and pride issue that Satan uses to recreate the things we fear most when we are vulnerable. What makes us more vulnerable than love? Not just the love of a person, but idols such as money, fame and respect. When we put any of these human wants before our relationship with God, it is a sin.

God had been putting the burden on my heart for me to quiet myself and learn to respond to things when prompted by Him, not to react to those around me out of fear or anger, so this relationship began to be a true test for me. Was I going to listen to what God wants for my life? Was I going to discern what is in line with his word and then follow his direction? Or was I going to give in to the fear and needs that had always ruled my life? As Victim Guy went through the book of James, I saw many changes in him, none of which seemed to be coming from a place of love or compassion, but more so from a place of judgment, bitterness, and an unforgiving spirit. It was all I could do to hold my tongue as accusations of my values and morals where being challenged. "Be patient and wait for God;" I told myself that God was faithful. It was not the answer I was praying for, but God asked me to follow Him; He showed me what love should look like and asked if this is what I saw in my relationship. Even though I wanted to ease my friend's pain, to love him enough that he would feel secure, I knew in my heart that this was exactly the role I always played. Rescue worker—that's me. Give me your wounded, give me your poor, give me your lost; I was playing God. Talk about pride and ego. I wasn't building a relationship, I was building up myself, and that is not being in love with someone. Having kindness, compassion or empathy for someone is not the same as being in love with that person. I think that eventually, the other person can sense the difference and that is what creates insecurity.

God had given me a heart for all those with whom I could identify: the wounded, poor and lost. But that did not make me in any way able to heal them from their demons. Even worse, I could distract them from God's work in them. That is what I was afraid was happening as I watched Victim Guy get more angry and frustrated that I would not bend to his need for me to walk with God in a way that made him feel safe and righteous. Truly, I think that we often give too much credit to our feelings for someone. How many time have we asked, if he or she really loved me he or she would . . . do what? Quit drinking? Quit being abusive? Stay on their meds? Get their life together? See me for who I really am? Feel secure? It's God's love that does all of this and more, not ours. In every relationship I have made excuses for the truth: that my relationships were based on lust first. Even in this relationship I had failed to follow God's scripture: As single Christians we are to abstain from sexual intimacy until marriage. This stands in contrast to the worldly perception of, "You've been married before. You're older it doesn't pertain to you. It's really about being in love with someone and not just having sex with someone." I knew that I was unsettled about this in the past and yet I fell again, and I will tell you truthfully that when I fell so did the relationship.

Victim Guy went from respecting me to treating me like every other woman in his life. I was now dishonest, untrustworthy, and sexually immoral; we went from him going to Church with me, waiting patiently for me, even becoming baptized in the Church, to him suspecting me of things I never even thought of. His actions ranged from going through business cards I had out on my counter and methodically laying them out so I would know he saw them, to accusing me of immoral behavior with my friends, including how I danced with them, even questioning a group picture that was taken years before we had even met. Everything became a trial: my clothing, my thoughts on disciplining children, even my motives in giving him time with his children. Everything was suspect or not enough. It was like sleeping with the enemy. Satan saw his open door and worked every comment, every action, and every thought to his favor. It wasn't long before it was no longer me standing in front of Victim Guy, I had become every woman by whom he felt victimized. He wouldn't open his own eyes to see his own sinful heart. He was too busy taking pride in his own education and "modality" in the field of mental health to open his eyes to the truth that we all play a part in our own self-destructive behavior, and no matter what the depth of the sin, addiction, lust, greed, pride, deception, manipulation, or slander, it is all equal in the eyes of the Lord and the only healer is Christ.

However, I had a decision to make. It was time for God to take center stage in my life, to truly put him first. So I followed God and I simply asked Victim Guy, "If I am truly the woman that you perceive me to be time and time again, then why would you want to be with me?" And with that I walked away from the relationship and I will tell you that it hurt so much; I was numb for a long time. I had it in my mind that I wanted that relationship to work. Outwardly it seemed to fit into my idea of what I wanted for my life, but God also has a plan for my life and I decided to follow His map. God made me profoundly aware that I have always put more importance on pleasing the men in my life instead of putting God first and moving at His pace so I can establish boundaries and feel safe to grow with someone. I have always given in—even when it didn't feel right—and I believe that there really is a method to God's teachings on waiting and being patient. To the expression, "good things come to those who wait," I will add, "for God's timing." I remind myself of this daily.

Throughout this time of separation I would go back to James to try to understand why God was using James to teach Victim Guy. Then, Pastor Tom, with his usual timing, announced that he would like to begin the book of James. I thought, "This is great—it will help Victim Guy find his way through this." I now know that it is not wise to look to God's teachings to move others before you look at yourself. One thing that Pastor Tom said was that a "wisely lived life is a fruitful life," and this stuck with me because I connected to the many references to planting, harvesting and the fruit of one's life. At that moment, the book of James came to life for me. Just as Jesus spoke in Matthew 13 from the parable of the sower through to the parable of the weeds, many will receive the word of God, and some will live it, some will use it, and some will walk away from it. But in the end, all will be gathered and separated by it. James revealed to me that the "seeds," or actions and behavior that we project, are exactly what we then gather. I recognized all that

I had gained through my past trials, as well as all that I had sacrificed with my poor choices, and that, if I wanted a different life, I would now have to learn to walk and talk in a new way. It also opened my eyes to those around me and gave me the ability to discern the truth from self-centered manipulation and how even our most socially-accepted desires lead us to sin. If we judge and do not show mercy, if we are proud and not humble, if we grumble and are not patient, but most of all, as in James 3:13-15: *If you have bitter jealousy and selfish ambition in your hearts, do not boast and be false to the truth. This is not the wisdom that comes down from above, but is earthly, unspiritual, and demonic. For where jealousy and selfish ambition exist, there will be disorder and every vile practice.*

One of the things I also saw in James was that the issues he was addressing to the twelve tribes are the same issues I run into in our communities today. The political wrestling to gain control over who gets more, who does more and the complete indifference to the idea of working together for the good of the community, all leads to a multitude of sin. Pastor Tom pointed out to us that James says that the fights and quarrels among us are caused by our protecting our own hidden desires or agendas. He said that we need to ask ourselves what we are trying to protect or gain: is it worldly treasure or Godly treasure? Then he went on to explain that a desire is a personal pleasure not for God and that a ruling desire takes that desire and elevates it to a sin or idol. This ruling desire reveals a deficient relationship with God. I knew that I needed God's mercy to overcome my deep need to be connected with someone, and that that deep need should be directed towards my relationship with Christ. I'm not sure what my connection to Marsha Burns' "Spirit of the Prophecy" is, but it seems to reinforce God's teachings and inspires me to hold on. My "Spirit of the Prophecy" on our last week of studying James read: "You've heard of the old adage, looking for love in all the wrong places. I say that many of, my people, are not only looking for love in the wrong places, but you are looking for answers in the wrong places. Try receiving love from Me, for it is an eternal love that will never disappoint. Try asking Me for wisdom, for I will answer every time. Try reading My Word to establish a foundation of truth in your heart, says the Lord. These are the right Places that will produce everlasting life, love, and peace," which was referencing James 1:5-8, *If any of you lacks wisdom, let him ask of God, who gives to all liberally and without reproach, and it will be given to him. But let him ask in faith, with no doubting, for he who doubts is like a wave of the sea driven and tossed by the wind. For let not that man suppose that he will receive anything from the Lord; he is a double-minded man, unstable in all his ways.* I was taken back to James 3:15, and with that, I listened as God called me to follow him, closing the book of James and my relationship and putting my faith and my heart in God's hands.

P.S. Note to self: It's probably not a good idea to play Melissa Gardner in Love Letters, and Marilyn Monroe for fundraisers nor Mary Magdalene in the Church play while dating an obsessive man. I keep playing Natalie Grant's "The Real Me" over and over, wondering if any one will ever see me for who I am, but also to remind myself the Christ knows the real me and more than that, He loves me!

Letters from Hosea

As my journey continued, God started to weed out those people, works and habits that He no longer wanted in my life, making them distasteful to my palate and replacing them with the sweetness of His glory. My brother and I saw God's work in our business as I was compelled to change the name to Noah's Ark and our new motto to "Navigating by Faith." It went from withering on the vine to producing a plentiful harvest. I felt His blessings everyday and couldn't wait until my ride to and from work to crank up my Christian music and sing out in worship to Him. He had taken over my life and I felt humbled that He would even think of me. Then one morning, I went straight to my email to open my daily devotional, The Spirit of the Prophecy, as I usually did, and that day's entry read, "Beloved, I am bringing correction to a specific course that began three years ago, which has been a transitional time in which you have had to make an extreme effort to stay in the divine flow of My purposes for you. Many times the battle became so fierce that you would have lost heart unless you had seen the goodness of the Lord in the land of the living (Psalm27:13). You have been in the Valley of Weeping. I have seen your tears and have been your only help in times of trouble. Now I have opened a door of hope where you will have breakthrough and rejoice in the progression of victory. I am giving you new strength for the journey before you says the Lord." Hosea 2:13-15 says, *I will punish her for the days of the Baals (idols) to which she burned incense. She decked herself with her earrings and jewelry, and went after her lovers; but Me she forgot, "says the Lord." Therefore, behold, I will allure her, will bring her into the wilderness, and speak comfort to her. I will give her vineyards from there, and the Valley of Achor (trouble) as a door of hope; she shall sing there, as in the days of her youth, as in the day when she came up for the land of Egypt.*

I wasn't quite sure of what to make of this. My journey through Ruth seemed to be over and I didn't feel drawn to one specific place in the Bible, and this just grabbed at my heart. I couldn't wait to get my hands on Hosea.

What I found there was a reflection that I never saw before. God stripped away the veil from the patterns of my life to show me that my thirst for love has only been quenched by temporary lust, not by true love. In the pain of my revelation, the thought that God saw me and my actions in this way just brought me to tears. In accepting social attitudes, even as a defense mechanism, by playing along with the flirtations, dirty jokes, and lewd comments of those around me, but more than that by accepting society's idea of a "committed" sexual relationship outside of God's plan of marriage, I had painted a picture of myself that jumped out of Hosea 2 so clearly. But in His mercy He once again offers me much more in His covenant with me in Hosea 16-20, *And in that day, declares the Lord, you will call me My Husband, and no longer will you call me "My Baal". For I will remove the names of the Baals from her mouth, and they shall be remembered by name no more. And I will make for them a covenant on that day with the beasts of the field, the birds of the heavens, and the creeping things of the ground. And I will abolish the bow, the sword, and war from the land, and I will make you lie down in safety. And I will betroth you to me forever. I will betroth you to me in righteousness and in justice, in steadfast love and in mercy. I will betroth you to me in faithfulness. And you shall know the Lord.*

I was in awe that through my belief in Christ, God was ever-present in my life to the point that He heard my heart's cry for peace from a battle that had taken everything from me: my strength, my wisdom and my confidence. I could hear the echoes of the past in my head, "No one will ever love you, after having stretch marks from having kids." "No nice guy would ever want to be with someone like you; he would be intimidated." "You dare to ask me to leave because I drink too much? I'm not your ex, hitting you and cheating on you, but I'm not good enough for you?" "No wonder the men in your life treat you the way they do." (That one was from Victim Guy; what a surprise!) It was the longest tunnel I had been through, one train wreck after another until I reached the other side, where I finally felt completely and totally loved for who I am with no conditions, no judgment, no grudges, just pure and simple love and forgiveness. Through Him, He has righted my wrongs and made me righteous because I am His. Once again He drew me back to 1 Corinthians 13:6 and showed me that a Christ-based love is not derived from lust; lust is contrary to everything that God wants love to be. Lust is self-centered, impatient, untrusting, unforgiving, controlling, shallow, demeaning and dries up the most loving heart. God then brought me to 13:11-13: *When I was a child, I spoke like a child; I thought like a child, I reasoned like a child. When I became a man, I gave up childish ways. For now we see in a mirror dimly, but then face to face. Now, I know in part: then I shall know fully, even as I have been fully known. So now faith, hope, and love abide, these three; but the greatest is love.* He once again lovingly and patiently showed His forgiveness to me and showed me that He did not hold judgment against me for when I did not know the difference between right and wrong, but now He asks that I give up those patterns and put my faith, hope and love in Him. Little by little God has changed the palate of my life regarding what I will allow into my presence. I find that the passing dirty joke, gossip, even the behavior that used to feed my soul is now tasteless and unappealing. I realize that God is alive in my life; He is constant to the point of relentless in His teaching, and most of all, He does hold me in the palm of His hand just as the potter holds clay.

P.S. The Casting Crowns song, "Does Anybody Hear Her," is just breaking my heart because I know that depth of pain. You wait and wait for your prince charming and you give in to the frog because you start to believe in anyone who pays attention to you. You deceive your heart into believing that this must be the one, and when he turns out to be just one more passerby you can't take back that part of your soul that you just gave to him, so there is a quiet death that dwells in you. I think I now know that the reason God asks us to be patient and wait until marriage for true intimacy is not a passing fancy but something you tend to and nurture so it will grow and flourish, producing strength and beauty with age.

Letters from Matthew

God initially used Matthew to introduce me to Christ. The very first scripture that called me on my journey was Matthew 16:15 when Jesus asked Peter, "Who do you say I am?" Throughout my journey I am drawn back to Matthew to support other scripture. I was also called to Matthew through a time of great trial, which once again brought gossip and slander upon me. Throughout my life I have been haunted by gossip, innuendo and outright slander; at times I let it break me and at times I laughed it off. Each time has left me more disillusioned about people, but this time God carried my burden. Being divorced twice, I had gotten used to people speculating about my personal life. Realizing that most people don't really know me even though they claim to, I had learned to distance myself from them and just continue to be myself while believing that in time, people would see the real me and not be so threatened. But I could have never predicted what was about to come.

After my recent break up with Victim Guy I had thrown myself into the expansion of our business and allowed God to inspire the transformation of it to the point of spending endless hours painting two of every kind of animal I could imagine. So I was completely caught off guard when I received a visit from a friend to tell me about the latest rumor that was going around. She somehow felt that it was her duty to tell me before anyone else, being my friend and all. It always amazes me when people actually go to the extreme of hiding their gossip with good intent. I always wonder what they are hoping to gain by such an act. I kept my composure and asked her what the motive was for someone to be telling such a lie about me to her, because I assured her that I would not accept slander against me. I told her that, as a Christian, I am offended by the comments, but I am also hurt and disappointed that after eight years of working to build a business in the city and after the hours of volunteer time I had put into bringing change to the city, from events, to guides, to beautification projects, the mere thought that my efforts could be so minimized due to someone's cowardly act of slander. It was unacceptable to me. I decided that I needed to wait on a response for this and put it in God's hands as I had really had enough of defending myself against lies. I'm a 46 year old grandmother who works endlessly between my business, my community and my house and I keep Sunday open for church and my family. My life is just not that exciting; I don't get the fascination!

Two weeks had passed and God had brought me to Matthew 15:19-20: *For out of the heart come evil thoughts, murder, adultery, sexual immorality, theft, false witness, slander, these are what defile a person.* God showed me that these were not things of my heart, but of those who had made claims against me. He asked me, "Who do I say you are?" and I answered, "I am yours." I always thought there was something I had done to cause such rumors, so I would allow Satan in to beat up my self-image by looking for the reasons why people would say such things. What God showed me was that rumors actually come from the evil in the heart of those who have proliferated lies, rather than rebuking them. He also took me back to James 3:14 and showed me the motives behind gossip so I looked into myself to see the truth. When any of us takes part in gossip we should first check our own heart to see what "lies" there. Our words are so powerful we can empower or enslave and we are accountable for every word. Matthew 7 says, *Judge not, that you be not judged. For with the judgment you pronounce you will be judged, and with the measure you use it will be measured to you. Why do you see the speck that is in your brother's eye, but do not notice the log that is in your own eye? Or how can you say to your brother, Let me take the speck out of your eye, when there is a log in your own eye? You hypocrite, first take the log out of your own eye, and then you will see clearly to take the speck out of your brother's eye.*

So I held on to the word until I received yet another helpful visit from another caring friend who let me know that this rumor was now on the local radio station. I just sat for a moment, dumbfounded, thinking. "This is crazy. Who would seek to persecute me in this way?" Quickly, before I relapsed and started questioning God's promises to me, which I had done so many times before, I stood on His authority in His righteousness and there I found peace. I kept my composure and called the station and asked what was said, and in what context this was even on the air, and who said it. Their response was of no help to me. They did not have a delay system or screening system so the airwaves were free to anyone to cast out any malicious accusations without regard for accountability. This is exactly what has brought our society to the state of vile voyeurism that is seen on television. I turned to the word and prayed for wisdom on how to handle this and I wrote out my feelings of anger and set it aside, and there it sat, waiting on Him.

Political leaders, attorneys and an outpouring of supportive community members came to me, everyone with their own thoughts on vindication and I refused to react. The one thing I knew was I did not want to respond in any way that would be negative for the community as a whole; I had worked too hard to build something positive that proclaimed the Glory of God in the midst of a society that is so jaded. God reminded me that those who choose to walk with Him are always under persecution: *Blessed are you when others revile you and persecute you and utter all kinds of evil against you falsely on my account. Rejoice and be glad, for your reward is great in heaven, for so they persecuted the prophets who were before you.* (Matthew 5:11). I have often found myself frustrated and suffocated living in Western New York. There exists such a pervasive negativity; everyone complains about everything but no wants to go through the discomfort of change. It is so discouraging that I have often wanted to walk away from it, but my heart belongs here. I see such beauty here with the majestic Niagara Falls, the Great Lakes that hand-carved the Niagara Escarpment, and miles of fruit trees and vineyards; every season brings new colors and tastes. Yet I fail to sell it to the very people who live here; I even co-founded a tourism campaign called DiscoverNYWest, hoping to open their eyes to all that they are blessed with every day, but that, too, became frustrating. I think for me, everything came to a head with this new round of accusations, I had had it. All I could do was keep reminding myself that God is faithful, that He will not forsake me, and to put it all on Him. As I did He brought me to Matthew 5:13-16: *You are the light of the world. A city set on a hill cannot be hidden, nor do people light a lamp and put it under a basket; but on a stand, and it gives light to all in the house. In the same way; let your light shine before others, so that they may see your good works and give glory to your Father who is in heaven.* I knew from those words that this was exactly where God had wanted me to be, in Western New York, in Grace Bible Church, at Noah's Ark, and I need to stand once and for all on Him.

Christ's continued calls of: "Follow me," took on a different meaning in Matthew 4:19: *Follow me and I will make you fishers of men.* After everything I had been through up to this point, I thought this probably is not the appropriate call for me. I'm thinking the last thing I want to do is cast a hook towards any man; I'm finally happy and at peace, I've watched as my own children started to question Christ as they saw the changes in me. My business has grown into something I never thought it could be and it brings me such joy, because I see Him in everything about it. I am blessed daily with customers who feel comfortable sharing their faith and I have even seen them come to Grace Bible. I have found myself so inspired at the growth and transformation that I run home, crank on the Christian music and dance with joy. I knew more than ever that it was time for me to walk away from serving a community and serve the Lord. I had known in my heart that God had wanted me to close the door on doing works for the world, but I guess my pride pushed me into saying yes to projects that, although they were with good intent, would never lead me to happiness. So God allowed me to struggle within my own strength to accomplish things that truly don't change anything when it comes down to it, because the only path to change is to humble oneself and truly follow the Lord.

With all that He has done, I also know that He knows the depth of my heart and my need to love others; I think that my need for attention came out of my need to connect with others, to see them smile, to laugh, to make them feel loved. So, as much as His words seem somewhat ironic to me, there they were calling louder and louder, *follow me and I will make you fishers of men!* It has been everywhere: on the radio, in the service, in casual conversations, even on a play rug I found for the playroom at the store. Now, I have never been shy about my conversations with God and His prodding, which generally all start the same: "Who, me?" "I don't think I can do this!" "I don't know enough: I'm not strong enough; there's got to be someone better suited for this; I know this drama is for your glory but I really can't sing!" But this time, all I could say is, "You've got to be kidding me!" I have grown to realize that even God has a sense of humor. He must; He listens to me sing every time I am in my car. I would like to say I know where this passage is going, but right now I am waiting with the greatest anticipation to see all that He can accomplish in me. I'm not jumping ahead or reading into it like I'm deciphering a code; I know that my faith is resting in Him and He will use the gifts that He has put inside me to His glory. His love and commitment to me inspires me to be more like Him every day in every way! I am Christ's work in progress!

P.S. I went to service this week which was given by our worship team leader about singing out in worship to the Lord. Pastor Scott closed with a request that everyone sing out and please feel free to offend. Hmm . . . . I think if there was one song I would sing, it would be "Today is the Day" by Paul Baloche: "Today is the day you have made, I will rejoice and be glad in it!"

Letters from Ephesians

This time Pastor Tom beat me to the punch. He started talking about going through Ephesians before I had finished Matthew, and before I knew it, I was in the throes of Ephesians. After months of praying for focus, direction and mercy for my wandering heart in those times when I yearned for someone to love, and to share my life with, I thought I had made great strides in my walk. I felt so blessed with all God had corrected in me and all that He had blessed me with all these years. So I was completely blindsided by the emotion I felt when I went to walk into church and Victim Guy came walking out with his new girlfriend. Now I had prayed that God would continue His work in Victim Guy and keep his family safe through their hard times, so I wasn't sure where my overwhelming feelings where coming from. The one thing I had always known about myself was that by the time I leave someone it is completely over (except for Miss the Boat Guy). I had learned to shut down my feelings and walk away. It's like in a play when the curtain comes down; that act is over and it is time to move on to the next scene. I never needed a Transition Guy to rescue me; I just distanced myself to the point that walking away was actually easier than staying. I think that my idea of love had become more of a performance than I had realized.

As I sat through the service my heart was so tight I couldn't breathe. At one point during worship I had to go out to get air. The sermon given by a church elder was called "Standing Firm on the Truth" and included Ephesians 6:10-14. When the service ended I sat there for a moment feeling numb and holding back tears and asking myself, "What is wrong with you?" Then one of the women from my grace group asked if I was okay and I answered with my typical response of, "I'll be fine; I'm just struggling a bit, but God is faithful." I must not have been very convincing, because she nudged me a little further. "I saw, (Victim Guy) with his girlfriend—are you okay?" And in that moment, God showed me that maybe I could trust someone besides myself to stand in Christ with me as I go through my challenge. After she had comforted me

I could feel God ease my fear of reaching out to someone and I went home thinking, "I'm okay; this is how God wants it and I am no longer going allow Satan to torture me with doubt."

When I left Victim Guy, I knew it was important not to react to him in any way that would allow Satan to feed his perception of women. I'm not sure why God put this so strongly on my heart, but He was very clear. He did not ask me, he commanded me; there was no way I was going fail in this. I could not let God down on this, no matter how many, "I should have said this" or "I should have said that" conversations I had with myself. I was not going to give in to my pain and anger. Yet, there I was standing in what felt like a pit watching my Christian Guy I had brought to the church, that I continued to pray for, walking out of my church with another woman. I swear that Satan was standing right at my side breathing down my neck with laughter. As I drove away from the church it was like my strength also slipped away and by the time I arrived home I was just broken. How could God forsake me after all this? As I sat at home crying my eyes out, I realized that I did not want to talk to any of my friends or even my sister about this, which is usually where I run to, because I really didn't think they would understand my sense of loss and betrayal; it didn't even make sense to me. So I reached out to my sister-in-law, who is the Christian woman poster child; she is amazing. In her worship, in her strength and even in her weakness, she glorifies God. We went to God's word and we didn't have far to go from service that day. Ephesians 6:10-14 said, *Be strong in the Lord and in the strength of his might. Put on the whole armor of God, that you may be able to stand against the schemes of the devil. For we do not wrestle against flesh and blood, but against the rulers, against the authorities, against the cosmic powers over this present darkness, against the spiritual forces of evil in the heavenly places. Therefore take up the whole armor of God, that you may be able to withstand in the evil day, and having done all, to stand firm. Stand therefore, having fastened on the belt of truth, and having put on the breastplate of righteousness.* As we hung up she told me she loved me, which of course made me cry again, but it was good.

I decided to sit quietly and reflect looking out over the lake; it was so calm it was like every wave followed my heartbeat. I had the need to read more of Ephesians so I grabbed my Bible and opened to 4:1-4: *I therefore, a prisoner for the Lord, urge you to walk in a manner worth of the calling to which you have been called with all humility and gentleness, with patience, bearing with one another in love eager to maintain the unity of the Spirit in the bond of peace. There is one body and one Spirit-just as you were called to the one hope that belongs to your call.* It goes on to point out to me that Grace Bible is not *my* church, it is *God's* church, and we as one body are only there by God's grace and only for His glory. His commitment to us is through our unity in faith He will bring us to maturity through the knowledge of Christ. In 4:14 Paul writes, *so that we may no longer be children, tossed to and fro by the waves and carried about by every wind of doctrine, by human cunning, by craftiness in deceitful schemes. Rather, speaking the truth in love, we are to grow up in every way into him who is the head, into Christ.* It amazes me that even when He corrects He makes you feel completely loved. I wish I could have known how to do that when I was raising my children.

There was so much there in Ephesians that spoke to me and reinforced God's purpose for me to spend this time on Him, not on pursuits of the heart or of the world, but to turn to Him in every moment of uncertainty. I received a message on my phone from the day before and it was our Grace Group leader wondering if I was going to make it to our meeting Sunday night and I smiled and I felt at peace. I went to Grace Group that night and shared my struggle. We prayed for each other that night, and as God would have it I gave one of the women there a ride home and we sat and talked for hours. God provided through the church body the peace that I needed. The following day I came into work and checked my Spirit of the Prophecy. It said, "Watch for definitive opportunities to overcome the works of the flesh through fear, failure and frustration. Be ready to resist the devil vehemently. New levels; new devils." It referenced Ephesians 2:1-5 which starts out: *As for you, you were dead in your transgressions and sins, in which you used to live when you followed the ways of this world and of the ruler of the kingdom of the air, the spirit who is now at work in those who are disobedient. All of us also lived among them at one time, gratifying the cravings of our sinful nature and following its desires and thoughts. Like the rest, we were by nature objects of wrath. But because of his great love for us, God, who is rich in mercy, made us alive with Christ even when we were dead in transgressions-it is by grace you have been saved.* I am continually astounded at God's love for me, that He would hold out His hand ask me to continue my walk with Him and say, for by grace you have been saved through faith in Jesus Christ.

Days later I shared my struggle with my sister and friend, both of whom are not sure where they stand in their faith. One is Muslim who was raised Catholic, the other a Unitarian Universalist. So I was shocked a couple days later when I received emails from each of them professing Christ. I was ministered to by the exact people Victim Guy said I should no longer be around. He said that God was telling me that I should only surround myself with Christians. Funny how he thought he could tell me what God was saying to me. The fact is that God has prepared me to walk in many lifestyles and feel comfortable, unafraid and most of all to stand against temptations other than those of the heart, that is. Once again I found myself back at Ephesians 2:4: *God, being rich in mercy, because of the great love with which he loved us, even when we were dead in our trespasses, made us alive together with Christ—by grace you have been saved.*" It goes on to say in 2:9-10: *"Not a result of works, so that no one may boast, For we are his workmanship, created in Christ Jesus for good works, which God prepared beforehand, that we should walk in them.* Even before I came to him he was working in me and he had made that very clear to me; He was there from my very beginning.

A few weeks later, I awoke to find my Satellite Dish out all but one station, BET, which had their morning worship programming on. I found a woman ministering on finding your identity in God and she went to Ephesians 1:11-12: *In him we have obtained an inheritance, having been predestined according to the purpose of him who works all things according to the counsel of his will, so the we who were the first to hope in Christ might be to the praise of his glory.* I grabbed my Bible and it was like God was standing in front of me asking me, "When will you commit your heart completely to me? Love me first! Let your identity and your happiness be in me not another. Walk in Love, but no longer walk with those who pursue deceitful desires, with hardened hearts or who give in to sensuality, but be an imitator of God. Let there be no filthiness nor foolish talk nor crude joking, those who are sexually immoral or impure or covetous have no inheritance in the kingdom of Christ and God. Let no one deceive you with empty words, take no part in the unfruitful works of darkness, but instead expose them. Stand in me, take up my shield of faith, take the helmet of salvation and the sword of the spirit and persevere in me, boldly proclaiming the mystery of the gospel. I held you through it all and will not let you fall." It's funny what God's word reveals about our own actions.

Growing up a tomboy in a small town, I really wasn't prepared for my metamorphosis into a woman. I didn't get what all the fuss was about; I still wanted to play ball, drive trucks and tractors, and build forts with my own tools, but the outside of me was attracting more attention than the inside of me knew what to do with. Even hidden under Carhartt coveralls, there was no stopping the sexual comments. It never seemed to matter what I did or what I wore it was always minimized by men and envied by women. I tried to laugh it off, be sarcastic, or ignore it, thinking if I can make them see who I am beyond this they will love me, but it never happened. At that point you get so sick of it that you buy in to their perception and decide to use it, sometimes leading you down dark roads and sometimes just playing along for a good cause. It doesn't matter what you do or how much you give; women gossip and men live under a delusion that their rudeness is flattering. Men also have the delusion that every woman wants them. How come women aren't that confident? No, not women. They are under the delusion that every single woman wants their man, which screams of insecurity.

The spirit of prophecy again brought me focus with the words, "My people, you will now begin to see the unveiling of a new order in My kingdom. In this time I will establish truth and justice, and in this process hidden indiscretions will come to light and will be judged, for you are entering a time of disclosure.

By the same token, those who have committed sins and have lost fellowship with Me will begin to seek to be restored to their kingdom position. Their restoration will depend on whether or not they are truly repentant. Those who have an ear to hear will begin to raise up a standard of spiritual and moral integrity for this new plateau. You will be required to question what you really believe, and thus define your doctrine more precisely. You will have to examine your code of ethics to make sure that your responses are consistent with the Word. Be on guard, for this new level of kingdom experience will be met with opposition from the enemy. This war will be called the Battle of Integrity as you face circumstances, situations, tests and trials that reveal your heart. War is always required to take new spiritual territory. I yield you to the work of My Spirit, you can win these battles one decision at a time as you establish and maintain integrity. You, My Church, are in a process of preparation, which will result in your being without spot and blameless, says the Lord." Ephesians 5:25-27 says, *Husbands, love your wives, just as Christ also loved the church and gave Himself for her, that He might sanctify and cleanse her with the washing of water by the word, that He might present her to Himself a glorious church, not having sport or wrinkle or any such thing, but that she should be holy and without blemish.*

All these years I've carried shame put on me by others' perceptions, but God has now given me the strength to stand in His righteousness to not receive false perceptions, accept unwanted advances, or tolerate idle talk. For the first time in my life, I can stand up for myself knowing who I am in Christ, with the assurance that God knows my name, and with a response that teaches rather than condemns. Again, I think of the song by Casting Crowns that says, "Not because who I am, but because what you've done, Not because what I've done but because of who you are." It reminds me that my righteousness comes through Christ and I am who he says I am.

P.S. One more note: Ephesians 5:19 says, "Address one another in psalms and hymns and spiritual songs, singing and making melody to the Lord with all your hearts." If this is God's command why do so many hymns sound like eulogies and why do we sit there emotionless when the Holy Spirit is calling us to rise up in song? Hmm.

Letters from Isaiah

I walked out onto the deck of my house and as looked out over the lake, there it was. God had sent me a rainbow that went right over my house and landed at the end of the pier. It was so vivid; its beauty and majesty reminded me of God's covenant with me. And I am in awe that He even cares that I exist, let alone that He is working in my favor at all times, which brings me to tears. The night before I had seen Victim Guy face to face at Bible Institute Class and God gave me such peace with the whole situation; He surrounded me with the body of Christ and for the first time I knew the meaning of a church family. He showed me that I had nothing to fear, that my judgment was necessary, that it was as simple as being obedient to His call. There was no need to look back, to second guess, or to feel uncomfortable, just prepare for God's plan for my life; that plan I can rest in his righteousness. My Spirit of the Prophecy for that day brought me to Isaiah 62:10: *Go through, Go through the Gates! Prepare the way for the people; build up, build up the highway! Take out the stones, lift up a banner for the peoples!* It said, "I have indeed opened a door before. You have been on the threshold and have now stepped through into a new dimension. There is no going back, ever! I have set before you revelation and life, life in the Spirit. Come through, come through the door. Come up, come up higher. Do not be afraid. Do not look behind you. Do not fall back into remorse or regret over the things you are leaving behind because I'm bringing you to new life, says the Lord."

I have found it almost charming that God has moved me through His word the way He has; it's a lot like a trainer luring a horse running in a pasture. Throughout my time on the farm I was blessed with many new friendships. One that made the biggest impression was that of my trainers Sue and Terry Williams, the owners of the Olympic gold medalist and World Champion horse Abdullah. What began as training a few horses led to starting a United States Pony Club and whole new world of fundraising, the "Horse Show." They opened my life up to a world I had never even dreamed of or seen in Western

New York, a world of extreme wealth and privilege. My experience of traveling to the Hampton Classic and The Winter Equestrian Festival in West Palm Beach was just a glimpse of the world they had seen with Abdullah, but what made me love them was that their humble beginnings never left them. Terry, the quintessential cowboy who found himself traveling in Europe and meeting heads of state in a second-hand tux, was the perfect yin to Sue's sophisticated and subtle yang. It was Terry who taught me to stand quietly and patiently with your hand out waiting to capture the heart of the horse instead of chasing after the horse until it is forced by the boundaries of pasture to submit. Of course, standing in a field with Terry was anything but quiet; it gave him time to pass on a lifetime of wisdom. I imagine Christ as our trainer standing out in a pasture with His hand out patiently speaking wisdom into our hearts as we finally submit, and that even in the brokenness of our life that often brings us to Him, He still wants us to freely choose Him.

Watching Sue and Terry with the horses, I was always amazed at the difference between horses that were forced into submission who would then spend their life fighting authority and reverting to their flight instinct any chance they got, and horses that were broken through the love, patience and guidance of a trainer who offered safety through consistency and companionship. That horse seemed to give so much more; people would often say, "That horse has such heart." I have prayed so often for help in getting into the word and understanding it, but it was so challenging and discouraging at times, that I would find myself standing in the pasture wondering whether I should run or submit. I finally chose to submit and asked for His guidance and my training began as He led me to small books, which I didn't even know existed, and reinforced it with larger books. It's almost like He knew exactly how my mind works, how much I can absorb at one time and how I need to almost immediately apply the things I read or I'll lose it. So I have gone through books like Matthew and Isaiah in baby steps, which makes it so much easier for me. There is such depth in these scriptures that my reading comprehension is truly challenged, but through His application and guidance He makes it come alive for me. I don't go in to it expecting an answer, I knock on the door and He answers as I find myself held captive in what was, what is and what will be.

This particular day I opened to Isaiah chapter 55, which starts: *Come all you who are thirsty come to the waters,* then goes on to reconfirm God's covenant with David. All I could picture was that rainbow that landed beyond the pier into the vastness of the lake. As I sat there taking in all that I perceived of God's word, I read, *My ways are higher than your ways, my word that goes out from my mouth, It will not return to me empty, but will accomplish what I desire and achieve the purpose for which I sent it,* and God pushed on and called my attention to 54:4. I was thinking to myself, "Wait! I'm not ready!" But popping up out of text like child's pop-up book came: *Do not be afraid you will not suffer shame. Do not fear disgrace; you will not be humiliated. You will forget the shame of your youth and remember no more the reproach of your widowhood. For your Maker is your husband the Lord Almighty is his name.* Then in 54:6 I was numbed by the words, *The Lord will call you back as if you were a wife deserted and distressed in spirit a wife who married young only to be rejected, says your God.* I was broken once more, my heart just wept and read on, *For a brief moment I abandoned you, but with deep compassion I will bring you back. In a surge of anger I hid my face from you for a moment, but with everlasting kindness I will have compassion on you, says the Lord your Redeemer.* The warmth and comfort over took me and I felt so loved. He continued, *to me this is like the days of Noah, when I swore that the waters of Noah would never again cover the earth. So now I have sworn not to be angry with you, never to rebuke you again. Though the mountains be shaken and the hills be removed yet my unfailing love for you will not be shaken nor my covenant of peace be removed.* As the hair on my whole body rose, my heart was at last healed. He held me up, like the rainbow in sky, washed me clean with the blood of His Son, and showed me clearly what love looks like. It is a commitment of unconditional love, built on the foundation of Christ with love, patience, respect, kindness and truth.

My spirit of prophecy read, "As you let go of the past and move to a new plateau spiritually, it will affect every area of your life. Expect change on every front, and be prepared to make decisions that will release you into new realms of experience and blessing. Yield to My Spirit, and I will take you higher. Do not be afraid to make the changes that present themselves to you for I am with you, says the Lord". Isaiah 42:16 says, *I will bring the blind by a way they did not know; I will lead them in paths they have not known. I will make darkness light before them, and crooked places straight. These things I will do for them, and not forsake them.* I was finally captivated by Isaiah; the writing sang out to me like a song in my head, like the rhythm of the waves against the shore of the lake. The continued reinforcement that I was right where God wanted me to be led me through a Christmas season that I could never have imagined. Through the endless stream of toy recalls and battles with outside forces, our little toy store grew in abundance, I had peace I had never known, and the frantic pace of life slowed for me to give thanks and praise to every moment spent with my family, church and friends. I had a security I had never felt, a love I had never felt and a strength that I never knew was there. My season ended with a spirit of prophecy in Isaiah 37:30-31: *This shall be a sign to you: You shall eat this year such as grows of itself, and the second year what springs from the same; also in the third year sow and reap, plant vineyards and eat the fruit of them. And the remnant who have escaped of the house of Judah shall again take root downward and bear fruit upward.* Marsha wrote, "Beloved, there are many things hidden that have not come to light. I tell you that these things are like seeds planted in the soil. They are putting down roots, but have not yet broken ground. From your vantage point it may look like there is no life, but not being able to see the manifestation of the planted seed does not mean it is non-existent. *The life is in the seed that you've planted, and soon you will see first the blade, then the head and after that the full grain in the head (Mark4:28)."* You will not only see the days of harvest of these hidden things but you will partake of their fullness and enjoy the multiplied blessing of this seed, says the Lord.

That gave me what I needed to write my first script for my Children's Christian Enrichment Show. I had been working a year and a half on developing it though I had never known where it was leading. I knew nothing else other than the fact that I was to write a show based on planting seeds, and with His hand, I did just that. With the Christmas season fast approaching, we were already experiencing such a great increase that I was physically exhausted. Against my better judgment, I had agreed once again to chair a Christmastime in the City, and there I was taking on the development of a children's Christian-based television show. At a time that looked like I truly was in over my head. I just sat numbly and said, "Lord if this is your plan show me how to accomplish it all, because I do not have the ability in my own strength to do all that is before me." The Lord, being the Lord of promise that He is, did not let me down. We saw more increase at the store than ever before, He brought the people to me that I needed to begin the show, and He helped me complete my commitment to the city. The biggest thing was that through it all He allowed me to experience the most peaceful Christmas I have ever known. I had such joy, contentment and focus; it was so contrary to who I was, always running in several different directions, never standing still long enough to see, feel and enjoy the fruits of my life, let alone to hear God's direction. Taking time to give thanks for those moments, I also realized that it was time to leave some things behind to focus on God's plan for me and to be open to where that will lead.

The Spirit of the Prophecy once again hit home when Marsha wrote, "a window has been opened in the heavenlies that will afford significant breakthrough in various areas of your life where you have needed conclusion and closure as well as opportunities for progress. Be aware of the favorable juncture of circumstances that will give you the ability to leave the past behind and press on. Rejoice in this shore season of release when you can refocus your energies and expectations, for certainly I have been with you even in the difficulties leading up to this time, and will continue to be with you to lead you in the flow of the next phase of your progression, says the Lord." Isaiah 58-11: *The LORD will guide you continually, and satisfy your soul in drought, and strengthen your bones; you shall be like a watered garden, and like a spring of water, whose waters do not fail.*

It's so funny that that was exactly what I felt when I would write the scripts for the show: reenergized and strengthened by this feeling that I was loved and not forgotten. I had a living God that calls out to me through my storms, that sees me with all my faults and will still stand beside me, and who lifts me up to see the gifts he has poured out on me. The one that was once unlovable, without talent or strength was finally whole, completely on my own, not through the love of a man but through His love alone. Who I am is no longer based on who I do and don't have in my life in this world; it is only based on what Christ did for me on the cross. He is my true savior. The Casting Crowns' song "I will Praise You in This Storm" really says it best, "I will praise the God who gives and takes away." It's easy to praise God when all is well, but to praise when you are breaking is love.

Letters from John

I have found that through my journey God has prodded and called and sometimes, as with John, just smacked me upside the head like a V-8 commercial. Everywhere I turned the book of John was coming at me on television, on the radio, in my Bible study. It was getting to the point of absurdity. At this time, I had become completely focused on working on the children's show. Every wall seemed to fall to the side as I passed through each obstacle, but it was clear that I was to go back to the word and also to my journal, so I once again let go of my need to stay on task and move to John. I'm still not sure why this journal of my journey is important, but I now know that it is somehow part of His whole plan and must not be forgotten.

What struck me right from the beginning was that the Gospel of John was different than the first three. It seemed like a more personal account, not in regards to the writer but to the reader. In one testimony after another, Christ spoke in love, kindness, truth and forgiveness to each of those who heard and followed Him. Even when there was a need for correction in behavior or a show of strength against persecution, He always responded in ways that taught and inspired one to transform his or her thoughts or behavior. In His humbleness He did not lord over people, but rather, he reached out with a hand asking, "Follow me." As I read each testimony, the Samaritan woman tugged at my heart. For the first time in my journey, the word did not bring me sadness and pain over the reality of my own sin, but a calm stillness. That was a picture of what was, I am the picture of what is and He is waiting to reveal picture of what will be. I was that woman standing before Jesus, a woman of promiscuity to whom He offered the living water, and I chose to drink from His cup. His commitment to me is that I will never thirst, that I will worship Him in spirit and truth. My commitment to Him is to follow Him, lean on Him and be a living testimony to His love. As the Samaritan woman shared her testimony and brought many more to Christ, so will I. Through His strength and forgiveness I can share even my most painful moments so that even one lamb might follow.

As I continued in John, I received my Spirit of the Prophecy and it read, "The devil is doing what he can to cause you to get overwhelmed with responsibilities and things that seem to be out of your control. This attack is for the express purpose of causing you to dismiss and let go of the promise of blessing in this season. You will have to work at holding on to the truth and keeping spiritual perspective at this time. Otherwise, the enemy can rob you. Do not let go of My promises, says the Lord, but rather make them your possession." John 10:10: *"The thief does not come except to steal, and to kill, and to destroy. I have come that they may have life, and that they may have it more abundantly."* I knew my heart was struggling in having to let go of all things I would do for the communities in which I lived or worked, and Satan was doing his best to play on my need to organize the world! Offers that I had long waited for were finally within my grasp; people were finally starting to see the vision I had always had. I felt so strongly that change would never happen if I didn't push people outside their comfort zone and into "Kathy Vision" as some of my friends call it. I have always been a doer, not a talker. Let's just accomplish something no matter how great or small, rather than sit around discussing it or doing a study on it. Let's just do it and keep developing it until it is what you envisioned.

After many years of being crucified in every way, shape or form, for all my "volunteer" work, I have come to the conclusion that the reason the Western New York area is so stagnant is that no one can let go of the past and move forward because to do so requires faith that God's plan will be greater than any plan of man. No matter how many people talk, whine or fight about it, sooner or later you must move towards growth or risk being choked out by the weeds beneath your feet. It also requires them to grasp the idea that not everything has to do with what's in it for them individually but that some things have to do with what's in it for the whole community. There is no other reason for the decline of a once prosperous area, because Western New York truly is one of the most amazing places to live. From the people to scenery, it's incredible. It is a great place to raise children; my own childhood was filled with the awe of adventures all across the County of Niagara and I know those memories are what kept me here. There is an old Irish proverb that says: *"You will never get a field plowed by turning it over in your head,"* so, to me, if God gives you a vision, you should pursue it with all diligence. So the stubborn Irishwoman in me was struggling to let go of the projects I had been working on, but God reminded me over and over that this was a season for me to stay focused on the work He had laid out for me. It was time to say no to distractions, no matter how tempting, and that is what I tried to do. Hanging up my chairman's hat and putting on the armor of Christ, I began to eliminate the weeds that Satan would plant around me. I went back to Matthew 13:24 when Jesus told the parable of the weeds and in Matthew 13:36 his explanation struck home for me: *"The weeds are the sons of the evil one, and the enemy who sows them is the devil."* I have to learn to be able recognize those things in my life that are not from God's Spirit and weed them out of my life in order to reach His garden.

Once again, I received great confirmation that I was moving in his path from the Spirit of the Prophecy. Marsha wrote, "Beloved, I will cause you to have the discernment to see and understand the things in your life that separate you from vibrant relationship with Me and produce spiritual death. Take a position of awareness and evaluate carefully all that you think and do to see what produces greater life, strength and growth. And, be willing to give up everything that does not generate health and vitality. Remember that I will show you these things as you seek Me for wisdom and direction, says the Lord." John 15:4-7: *"Abide in Me, and I in you. As the branch cannot bear fruit of itself, unless it abides in the vine, neither can you, unless you abide in Me. I am the vine, you are the branches. He who abides in Me, and I in him, bears much fruit; for without Me you can do nothing. If anyone does not abide in Me, he is cast out as a branch and is withered; and they gather them and throw them into the fire, and they are burned. If you abide in Me, and My words abide in you, you will ask what you desire, and it shall be done for you."*

Wow, sometimes God is so crazy! After I had written the above, I thought my walk through John was introspective (or should I say "all about me") and then Pastor Tom said we would spend Easter "walking through the book of John." So I asked myself, what is it that I am not seeing or hearing clearly? It seems that in midst of my transformation I was not listening to what God was showing me in my own Church body as well as my new life with the body, because now we are one, joined by Him to glorify Him. I have become so used to being someone who was always on the outside looking in at relationships of others that it dawned on me that maybe the distance between us was really only as thin as the pane of glass I was looking through. I wondered if maybe God has allowed me to walk in the path of so many on my journey to Him, so that I could feel their pain more deeply, as though it where my own. I knew the struggle of poverty, of single parenthood, of abuse, of disability, of scorn and ridicule, of rape, abortion and the constant temptations that put you in a hamster ball forever running to nowhere, surrounded by a translucent wall that isolates you from the truth. Maybe now is the time for me to stop running around and around inside the security of the walls of that hamster ball. God has patiently prepared me for this time; I am no longer orphaned by my sin, but rather I am loved by a great God, and I am a wanted heart!

In service Pastor Tom spoke of Psalm 51 in which David writes, *For I know my transgressions, and my sin is ever before me. Against you, you only, have I sinned and done what is evil in your sight, so that you may be justified in your words and blameless in your judgment. But he also says; Deliver me from bloodguiltiness, O God, O God of my salvation and my tongue will sing aloud of your righteousness. O Lord, open my lips, and my mouth will declare your praise.* What had always held me captive was the weight of my sin, but in John, Christ showed me that the heart of the world we live in is not far from the heart of the nation Christ walked in. In the same way that the Pharisees question Christ's forgiveness of the adulterous woman and rebuked Him in the healing of the blind man on the Sabbath, so did His own disciples question His speaking to the Samaritan woman and Mary anointing His feet. We all stand on one line of the scripture or the other: the side that believes that we have a powerful and loving God who gave us salvation through His Son and who lives in us through the Holy Spirit helping us to attain His plan for our life, or the side that minimizes all He is, questioning and rebuking all change so that we can maintain control.

Pastor Tom has said many times that if you see something repeated in the scripture it is strengthening the message. I think that is also true when you hear repeated references to topics of conversation. So when references to churches who become divided over scripture or even music kept popping up, I noticed a change in the church. I kept thinking, "Now scripture, I can see as challenging, but music?" Then I realized it really wasn't about music choice, it was just a way to minimize the person's voice, and control the passion of worship. I never really gave it a lot of thought; once I went to a Pentecostal Church with Charismatic Christian Guy, and I realized then that there are many ways to worship Christ, but the most honest way for me was to wait on the Holy Spirit to guide my heart, because I felt that anything else would not be truthful. I've gotten to a point in my life in which I have been through these things so many times, where someone sparks a flame of change and all the people in charge of keeping a hold on status quo jump to put a lid on it without thought to where the flame may lead. The true leader must learn to lead people where they need to go, not where they want to go, because that requires them to come out of their comfort zone and only then will they truly grow.

I wonder if God would look at us as Pharisees as we try to control worship or who should teach and who should lead. I thought God called each of us to be His own, and that we should worship, minister, teach and love others as Christ loved us. Doesn't minimizing God's gifts, just make Him a small God? I do not understand God's selection process, but I will not minimize His call on my life. God made us all one; male, female, black, white, thief, addict, and murderer—we are all one through Christ. I do not understand the gifts He has put in me let alone the gifts I see in others, but I will never again minimize them according to my own understanding. It is He who creates, He who strengthens, He who feeds through ways that are His alone, and not of my understanding. John 14:12 says, *Christ says truly, truly I say to you whoever believes in me will also do the works I do and greater works than these.* The Psalms written by David, the man after God's own heart, who danced in the streets in his undergarments to worship his glorious God, should be the example we all hold in our hearts: to Love our God with all our hearts, in song and praise and worship. Add to that, loving your neighbor as yourself, and we can all rise in dance as one! I am reminded of the first time I heard the song "I can only imagine." I was in my horse barn in my Carhartts, and even though at that time I was still lost, I couldn't help but dance. It was the one gift I knew God had given me. What greater pleasure would there be than to dance for Jesus?

Maybe I see things differently because my life has brought me through the lowest of lows and the highest of highs from poverty to riches and yet I see through the eyes of those who struggle no matter what their status is. I see my friends who have been blessed with so much lose touch of their humble beginnings and forgiving heart. Buying in to a world-view of materialism that, in their minds, gives them the right to be judgmental, slanderous and unforgiving, even as they suffer pain from their own sin, they still will not look in the mirror. What is the fear in us that drives us to minimize another's thoughts or feelings without first listening with the heart of Christ and responding in a way that supports growth even if it requires us to change? I used to put the responsibility on myself when I would run into this with other women, in business, politics or even my own relationships. I used to tell myself it was just jealousy, that they're just intimidated by me, it's the good old boys club again, and then Christ showed me that it really just comes down to lack of faith that God is in control and that His plan is greater than man's and it can be worked through all who believe in Him and even those who don't yet believe.

In John, Christ worked through Nicodemus, a ruler of the Jews, a Samaritan woman who was promiscuous, An official at Capernaum, an invalid, the lame and paralyzed, and in the man born blind. When questioned about the blind man being blind due to sin, Jesus answered, *It was not that this man sinned, or his parents, but that the works of God might be displayed in him.* When Lazarus had died and Christ had raised him from the dead, his death was a testimony to God's presence in every detail, even those details that bring pain, loss and suffering, because through Christ we will rise again for the greater glory of God. Lazarus, the brother of Mary Magdalene, the woman who chose to follow Christ all the way to the end, even some of the chosen disciples were not there as He hung on the cross, but Mary was. The woman who Judas scorned for using expensive ointment to anoint the feet of Jesus, the woman that Pope Gregory, marked as a prostitute and adulteress in 591 A.D. even though there was no evidence of that in the Gospel, the woman that even today authors continue to condemn as having an improper relationship with Christ was there. Why? Why can't it just be that she was called to follow Him and she did, with all her heart, with all that she had to give? It states in the Gospel that she had seven demons driven out from her. Throughout the Bible there is one thing that I find consistent: once one is called by name that is it, there is no guessing. Also when one is called out on their sin they are called out. It is not minimized by saying he had a battle with a demon; it is clear that one was a drunkard, an adulterer was an adulterer, a murderer was a murderer, a prostitute was a prostitute, a wife was a wife, a lover was a lover. Yet, I can find nothing to paint Mary Magdalene as anything but a devoted follower of Christ who gave to His ministry and in her own words called Him teacher. Christ chose to reveal Himself at the time of resurrection to Mary first out of everyone who followed Him, and she called Him teacher. Not my love, husband, or even my master, but my teacher. His response was not one of a lover, but that of a teacher, "Go and tell that I am ascending to my Father." Yet the sinful heart of the world would rather minimize her strength and knowledge of Christ to that of a lustful relationship. It could not have been simple respect and love for a woman, who, while others would deny Him, would stand at the foot of the cross, and then go to prepare His body after His death. I honestly don't think that I could have watched all that unfolded. I can't even get through "The Passion of the Christ" and I know it's a movie.

I never expected that I would find all of this in the Book of John; the revelation that I am feeling in my heart is sadness and a sense loss that the world has not changed that much in two thousand years. Even in today's Church, the voices of many go unheard, the calling of Christ on their heart is minimized, and the weight of their sin is measured as unforgivable. Did Christ come to take our sin, to make us all one before the Father, or didn't he? As Christ has walked me through both the Old and New Testament, it seems as though He keeps reinforcing to me that God calls us all, in His time, to His glory, to minister to those in need, to love the unlovable, and most of all to show them the heart of His spirit through worship. So are we to sit in silence and be obedient to laws that don't exalt Him? I don't see the Fruit of the Spirit in this. God is the only one who has the power to oppress, not man. All throughout history oppression has led to anger. It was Christ in John 19:30 who said, *it is finished*. So shouldn't we look at each other as Christ looked at Mary, and she at Him, not with sinful hearts but as sister and brother? As Christ died on the cross did not the bitter fruit of sin fall from Adam and Eve's mouths and be replaced by the Fruit of the Spirit? It was also Christ who promised to send the Spirit of Truth to be our counselor and He did so with blazing tongues. How can we be on fire to minister to those who have not heard if we are worried about rising up in worship in front those who have heard? The funny thing about all of this is the reason I felt so drawn to Grace Bible was the you could actually feel the presence of the Holy Spirit as Pastor Tom spoke, it would just pour down on him like an all-out rain sprinkling all who heard with the strength and wisdom needed for the week ahead. I'm not sure where this change is heading, but I trust that it is all according to His plan and that at the end of this tunnel

He stands with arms wide open. I have faith that He hears all of His children now as He did the children of Israel, and that He knows the way and will in time lead us all home, so I can rest in God's promise and continue to pray for our leaders in the world and in the church. I also know that I do not have to react to this moment; I should now more than ever respond, offering by only the Fruit of the Spirit and wait for a greater harvest.

I went to church this week with a group of my friends. It was uplifting to know that it was true that God was not asking me to leave my friends behind as I walked on my journey, but to share my path with all the love and joy He has brought to my life. In service Pastor Tom spoke of unity in trying times. Even though we were still going through Ephesians, he went to John 17 and this time I knew for me this chapter was over. It ended with Christ's prayer for those who follow, those who lead, and those who teach. That is what I must do: pray. I must pray for strength in challenging times for all who are called by Christ to lead, because this is the broken world that we have been called to minister in.

Just as I suspected, I should be still and wait on him! Today my Spirit of the Prophecy read, "You have faced and dealt with many challenges, and I know your heart cries out for closure and resolution. But, I tell you that this transitional time of bringing order out of chaos is not yet finished. There are still issues that must be settled before you can move on. Even though your involvement in these situations has caused you to believe that it is all about you, the truth is that everyone involved is being aroused to greater spiritual integrity, which is the order of the day. This is not only about you! Be patient as you maneuver your way through this maze of motives, behaviors and actions, and you will soon be released to a new level of spiritual accountability and truth, says the Lord." 1 John 4:6: *We are of God. He who knows God hears us; he who is not of God does not hear us. By this we know the spirit of truth and the spirit of error.* Amen!

P.S. Casting Crowns has a song called "I am Every Man." It sums up what I feel right now. All that I have been through and accomplished as a single mom has led me to a profound feeling of walking in the shoes of all who suffer, all who survive and all who, when push comes to shove, can now stand strong in Christ. So I am thankful for roads that lead me to Him no matter how twisted.

I received my Spirit of the Prophecy today and even though God has called me to Revelations, I believe this best fits what Pastor Tom addressed in Ephesians 4 on Sunday: "I have been hearing the word connectivity in my spirit over the past few days. Connectivity is the ability to make a connection and the state of being connected. And, the Lord says: The enemy is challenging and hindering your ability to make and maintain spiritual connections. This attack is first intended to separate you from Me, says the Lord, and additionally to bring division between My people, for he knows that if you will stay connected and unified his work of destruction is thwarted. Yours is to defeat the devil's purposes by staying connected." Ephesians 4:1-6: *I, therefore, the prisoner of the Lord, beseech you to walk worthy of the calling with which you were called, with all lowliness and gentleness, with longsuffering, bearing with one another in love, endeavoring to keep the unity of the Spirit in the bond of peace. There is one body and one Spirit, just as you were called in one hope of your calling; one Lord, one faith, one baptism; one God and Father of all, who is above all, and through all, and in you all.* My faith is in Him, who put me here for His purpose and for this time; whatever He calls me to do, I will follow. It is the fortieth anniversary of the death of Martin Luther King, Jr. I have such a sense of loss when I reflect on a time that I do not even remember, but sadly the call for unity, hope, peace and love is still just an echo, even in God's Church.

Pastor Tom attended our Grace group this week to address the conflict that had caused so much pain and strife within the group. It is hard to watch struggle among those for whom you know the Lord is in their hearts; it just shows me that we cannot be complacent in our prayer, because none of us, even leaders, are above attacks that challenge them to walk in a Christ—like manner. It is humbling when God uses others to show us our own need for growth and change. It is very stressful to feel confident in what God is asking of me in this circumstance; it was hard to even voice my own hopes for resolution and my faith that God is, as always, sovereign, even in this moment. Let those who have ears to hear keep coming to me. One great thing about what God has revealed to me is that all of the attacks and persecution I have faced throughout my life have allowed me to rest in Him and allow Him to bring me through the storm. I no longer have the need to be right because He has made me righteous in His ways. It makes me wonder if we are really ready to minister to those who will challenge the authority of the scripture if we are so crushed in the moment of conflict in our own body. I think sometimes it is not enough to take people to scripture for discipline or rebuke; you must give an example of that sin in the given moment and lead with a heart of forgiveness. Christ had this way of dealing with sin and it just humbled even the hardest of hearts, Paul's for one, mine for another.

I was not surprised—the next morning, the Spirit of the Prophecy read, "Be careful that you do not misread or misinterpret the signs of the season. Chaos is succumbing to order in ways that you have not yet thought of. This work is by My Spirit and will require you to be willing and flexible. Do not rebel against this important work or become stubborn or hard-headed, but rather yield quickly. If you will discern My plans and purposes, you will be able to see the larger picture and know that this transformation is not just about you. It has to do with you as a part of the whole. Go with the flow, says the Lord." Ephesians 4:11-16: *And He Himself gave some to be apostles, some prophets, some evangelists, and some pastors and teachers, for the equipping of the saints for the work of ministry, for the edifying of the body of Christ, till we all come to the unity of the faith and of the knowledge of the Son of God, to a perfect man, to the measure of the stature of the fullness of Christ; that we should no longer be children, tossed to and fro and carried about with every wind of doctrine, by the trickery of men, in the cunning craftiness of deceitful plotting, but, speaking the truth in love, may grow up in all things into Him who is the head—Christ—from whom the whole body, joined and knit together by what every joint supplies, according to the effective working by which every part does its share, causes growth of the body for the edifying of itself in love.* I'm not sure how Ephesians goes with John, but it seems to go hand in hand just like every testimony in the Bible, one leading to the other, in perfect time. God's timing.

Well, with diligence, God showed me John's tie to Ephesians. It was in Ephesus where John had lived in his later years and where he took on the false teachings that Paul had warned of in Ephesians. In John MacArthur's commentary, I had a strong feeling familiarity from our Grace group's recent struggle to come together as the Body of Christ during an attack on the church's beliefs. MacArthur says, "A lack of love for fellow believers characterizes false teachers, especially as they react against anyone rejecting their new way of thinking. (He references 1 John 3:10-18) They separated their deceived followers from the fellowship of those who remained faithful to apostolic teaching, leading John to reply that such separation outwardly manifested that those who followed false teachers lacked genuine salvation." (2:19) "Their departure left the other believers, who remained faithful to apostolic doctrine, shaken." This was the breakdown that unfolded before the group and it was Pastor Tom who brought the flock back to unity through the Word. What I admire in those Christian men I see dedicated to the truth is a humbleness that can calm the waves even in a storm. They don't work to stir up the ocean or to strike back out of pride, but rather, they put all faith in God's covenant with us that He will never flood the earth and they stand firmly holding back the winds, allowing God to do His work so that His tide of change can usher in growth. This was my first introduction to MacArthur's Commentary, and I found it amazing that this book was brought to me at this time to be used in a Bible Study at the restaurant my friends own. This is like the "Cheers" of Wilson and this is the very group of friends that Victim Guy said God was telling me to stop being around.

P.S. Victim Guy came to Church once again with another new girlfriend. After taking her to the restaurant to apparently introduce her to my "immoral" friends, then using the pier behind my house as "make-out point", I knew that he would be sitting behind me at church that Sunday, and I was right. I asked myself what God was trying to reveal to me in this, because I know that He is a sovereign God and He would not put me in a situation that served only to hurt me. What was funny was that this time, I really wasn't hurt, I felt comforted as I waited for my answer. My answer was that like Esau, I had sold my inheritance for the temporary comforts of this world; like David I had counted myself righteous in the pursuit of passion; like Judas I had rebuked my teacher to gain favor with those of the world. I am a sinner. "I am every man." My God is a merciful and loving Father who sent His Son to accept the wrath of my sin upon Himself, leaving me as white as snow. His Spirit dwells in me, teaching me, correcting me, leading me. My God is alive in His word, and I am thankful for another twisted road made straight!

Letters from 1 Corinthians

It somehow seems that a trip to Corinth is in order, although for the first time in my life I seem to be able to understand the book of Revelations. I am reading through it like eating through a piece of cheesecake! For some reason I feel intrigued by Corinth and the condition of the city at the time Paul wrote his letters. Corinth was a church that was formed by idolaters, adulterers, prostitutes, thieves and drunkards: it seems to depict today's world. I fear the cost to our children being exposed daily to things that I cannot conceive of at my age, let alone as a young child. The one and only thing that has motivated me in my life is children; they are the one thing that can make me laugh through tears. They bring me such joy that I can't watch them play without welling up with tears. I cannot even go to see dance recitals without getting a lump in my throat. To me they are such an incredible gift; everyone seems to search for their natural gifts in external things like, art, music, sports. As for me, I think the best gift is spending time running around barefoot in the green, spring grass, surrounded by the laughter of children, as spring peepers sing and the smell of flowers and fruit tree blossoms wafts through the air.

At Grace Group our leader asked each of us what we thought our gift was, and this is a question that just bugs me. I remember standing in front of the Baron of Branding when I had helped organize an event to showcase his renovation on the Wilson Harbor. He was in his own right a very successful man who had a huge heart for this little harbor that he purchased and then truly made it an amazing destination place. He stood on the dock and said to me, "You have a gift in organizing events—you're a creative person; I would just like to see you be more left-brained." I was biting my tongue, thinking, excuse me? Trying to hold myself back from pushing him off the dock, I smiled. He continued to explain that he was also more right-brained and that's why he hired other people to support his creativity. At that moment I thought he was actually brainless, but I reminded myself that men and women do not speak the same language. See, in woman language he was saying I had half a brain, and being a woman who has had to fight to get people to look beyond the outside of me to hear the inside of me, his comment was irritating. Not to mention that I never saw myself as someone who was talented or gifted. I just looked at something that needed to be accomplished and just did it. It was never some spiritual thing that I just knew, or was good at. They were just things that were ahead of me that I needed to complete. I would go to whoever the source of the knowledge was that I needed and I would learn from them; it was never my gift, it was more of a trade that I had worked my butt off to learn. I think when someone says you are gifted it means that something comes natural to you, like Mozart or Van Gogh. I haven't found anything that I am naturally talented at so I guess all this talk about giftedness bewilders me. I see non-Christians who are as naturally talented as Christians so I have to believe that God's spiritual gifts must be greater or different than those.

As Paul lays out the guidelines of the church to Corinth, he clearly speaks of everything from God's gifts to proper behavior and dress. It is amazing to me that people get hung up on speaking of tongues, healing, and the gift of prophecy or even whether or not women should teach in the church. It's like they want to pick and choose what scripture is true today, as if we are so much more evolved than they were two thousand years ago. They can say woman don't have to cover their heads, but still must be submissive and cannot teach. I was so moved by the whole head covering thing I decided to commit forty days to submitting myself to God's call to wearing a covering. I thought, "Well show me the difference, if my head is cover do I think differently, act differently, what?" I blogged about my experience for forty days and it actually did change my perspective on Paul's writings. After that experience, I didn't look at his writings in the same way. I no longer thought he wrote to make women less in the eyes of men, but actually more. What I experienced was more respect from those around me, not less. So, ladies, maybe less is not more in the eyes of men; maybe respect is given according to the mysterious and not the obvious.

Paul gives specific instructions on spiritual gifts, but some of today's churches don't believe the gifts exist anymore. For me, I have faith that God is everything He says He is in the Bible. He can call people to heal, call people to prophecy and even call woman to teach if it's His will. He used women in many ways throughout the Bible; they were not forgotten chattel. As for tongues, I am not threatened by anything that is from the Holy Spirit, but I believe that God will use all His gifts just as He instructs, and any use of any gift outside of God's instruction is false teaching. I believe that if God wanted me to speak in tongues, I would. Knowing how much I already speak in my own tongue, He probably doesn't think it's necessary. I love how Paul writes in 1Corinth 14:22-25, *Thus tongues are a sign not for the believers but for unbelievers, while prophecy is a sign not for unbelievers but for believers. If therefore, the whole church comes together and all speak in tongues, and outsiders or unbelievers enter, will they not say that you are out of your minds? But if all prophesy, and an unbeliever or outsider enters, he is convicted by all, he is called to account by all, the secrets of his heart are disclosed and so falling on his face he will worship God and declare that God is really among you.*

The truth is that I don't feel the need for God to lavish me with any natural or supernatural gifts to prove to me that He loves me, or to make me feel special in His eyes, I feel blessed that, with all I've been, He would even call me, teach me and hold me. Gifts or no gifts does not bring my heart any closer to Him, does not make my faith any stronger, and does not make me more or less in His eyes. I see the work He does in my life every day. I pray that I may be obedient and respectful to His word, and that He may give me correction and discernment in all areas including legalism versus truth and the heart of Christ.

My Spirit of the Prophecy reminded me today to, "Listen to the sound of the wind of My Spirit as I whisper the direction of your destiny. Be still and shut out the loud, abrasive voices that bring confusion and disarray so that you can indeed hear My still small voice. You are about to take a turn for the better, but you must leave behind the troubles of the past and look forward with anticipation to the things that I have prepared for you, says the Lord." 1 Corinthians 2:9: *But as it is written: "Eye has not seen, nor ear heard, nor have entered into the heart of man the things which God has prepared for those who love Him."* It is such a struggle to not fall back into my old ways of thinking but to stay focused on Him and to allow Him to move through me to once and for all close the doors to my past and maintain hope for the future that He will provide all that I need. I sometimes fear that I will not have the right words to say to those who need to hear. I often find myself in tears over the thought that I could add one thing to someone's life that would make them seek for themselves and then I am reminded by Paul in 1 Corinthians that it is not about my wisdom, my eloquence or anything that I do or bring, it is about what God put in me through the Holy Spirit. I can rest knowing that His words are enough for anyone to hear. I had so many fears in bringing the children's show to fruition: that I could not possibly be able to bring the context of the word to a format that would be enough to bring Him glory, and I was right. It wasn't me, I was just the tool He used, He brought the story through me, like an author holds a pen, a painter holds a brush, a musician hold an instrument, or a carpenter holds a hammer. He put the vision there long before I could see, He put the passion there even though I was numb, and carried me step by step in the palm of His hand until the work was done. Today I watched the very first completed show and there right in front of me was my heart, wide open, every moment of my life—every piece of the puzzle was brought together for His glory, and it was good.

The next day I received my Spirit of the Prophecy and I read: "I am opening a great effective door of evangelism for you, but you will not be able to go through using religious techniques that have been established through what you have been taught. This will be a move of My Spirit like nothing you have ever experienced. I have equipped you and prepared you, and now you will be able to go forth with a pure heart and attitude that will not bring attention to yourself and your ministry, but it will only bring the revelation and glory of My kingdom. Only the humble in heart will be able to go through this door of opportunity, says the Lord." *1 Corinthians 16:9: For a great and effective door has opened to me, and there are many adversaries.* I know that I will face criticism for the show because that is what the world does: they criticize what they do not know or understand. What they do not know is that no one could be more critical of my ability to lead in God's word than myself, because I truly know that I am unworthy of such a calling.

I know that, even now, my heart is not faithful, even with all that He has shown me; still, I am as a grieving child, yearning for something that has long since passed. God has shown me in every way that He has called me to be single, and yet my heart breaks instead of rejoicing as Paul did in 1 Corinthians 7:8: *To the unmarried and the widows, I say that it is good for them to remain single as I am.* I cannot see through my own desire to find completeness in serving Him, and that hurts my soul. Paul says we should celebrate in our singleness for the opportunity to be completely devoted to the Lord, but as hard as I try I can't get over feeling like someone just ran over my dog with a car. I love serving; it brings me a joy that I've never known before. It's different than all the volunteer work I've done. I think the difference is that in serving the Lord you are not serving the worldliness of others and there is a great peace in that. There is no power struggle, no being taken for granted, or deceptiveness to blind you. He is who He says He is and does all things for His purpose. I don't want to be like the Israelites mourning their old life of slavery because the road to the freedom God promised is hard and dry, fraught with hunger, and war. I would rather be like Paul who didn't just endure his suffering but found a greater joy in his sacrifices for Christ.

I have gone so many times to 1 Corinthians in search of direction and comfort that it is like visiting an old friend. I am once again reminded that as a part of the body of Christ, I must respect the human body that is now His temple. He dwells in me, so all that I do against my body, I do against Him. The same is true that all that I do as part of the Church body should be to glorify God and nourish the body with Christ's spiritual fruit. I think what Paul tells us in 1 Corinthians is that in all things, relationships, worship, teaching, praying, interaction with each other, we are called to love as Christ loved his Church, speak as Christ spoke to all who sought him out, in kindness and self-control, walk as Christ walked with all humility, and put Unity above our own pride and comfort. For Christ laid it all down on the cross that we would know that, our God is the God of promise, of resurrection, and eternity. Amen!

I went to church this week knowing that once again Victim Guy would be there with a new girl, his pattern is so obvious it is now ridiculous. Last week he came alone after an absence following the last girl, again showing up to introduce this girl to my friends. So as it would be, I walked in to church as he was walking out, we exchanged hellos, and I honestly was exhausted with it. My struggle the past week with being single and wanting so desperately to not long for anyone, to be content and at peace with where God has asked me to be was difficult enough. I really didn't feel as though I needed to be reminded again of my sin in that relationship. I have stayed focus on work and the word and turned away from anyone who tries to divert my attention. I have worked to change all those feelings, emotions, and activities that could lead me down the wrong road again, and at this point I am honestly tired. I am completely frustrated with myself that I just can't cut that part of my heart out so it would finally stop bleeding into my mind. I have a ridiculously romantic heart that has no sense of reality when it comes to falling in love.

I think part of the reason I love being with kids and doing parties for them is that I can create a fairytale for them. I can watch them smile, and laugh, sing and dance, and in that moment I feel loved. Like Julia Roberts in *Pretty Woman*, I kept waiting for the fairytale, but the reality is that fairytales are unrealistic expectations of life imitating art.

I wrote a note to myself in church last week. I should have known it was going to be a tough week because it said, "Why can I not be obedient like Christ to the point of death? Can I not make You my whole-hearted passion and not be bereft? Lift the idol of my heart because all other love creates a cleft." Who rhymes a word like cleft at church? By cleft I meant divide, because that is what it feels like: that any relationship I would have right now would leave me empty and divided between what I know the word says and the intimate nature or expectations of partners today. Even Christian men don't walk the walk anymore. There is no longer a respect for purity between two people; there is only a desire to bend God's word to make our wants, and our needs socially acceptable. I don't want to be double minded in this issue, because I believe God's reasons for waiting are completely for our own good. Pastor Dave said this week that God will only ask us to do what will be good for us, even though it is uncomfortable for a while, so that it will lead us to true freedom from our sin. Then when we are truly free from our sin we are free to pursue holiness and righteousness through Christ. He spoke of 1 Corinthians 9, 24-27 where Paul uses a metaphor for spiritual discipline as an athlete training to run a race to attain a crown of wreaths or a boxer throwing punches in the air. *We need in all ways to practice self control to attain victory for an eternal crown, not one that will wither away but be everlasting for the kingdom of God.*

Something funny happened this week at Church. A man stopped me as I was getting ready to leave and introduced himself, saying, "I don't usually do this . . ." (which is always a nightmare address for me), "but I notice that you seem burdened today and I don't know why but I was compelled to speak to you. I apologize and I don't mean to pry, but I just want to make sure you're okay." It made me kind of laugh inside because I knew God was using him to let me know He knew my struggle. So as we spoke he said, "God is faithful, and He will not let you be tempted beyond your ability." I smiled with a new confidence, because that is from 1 Corinthians 10:13. The whole verse says this: *No temptation has overtaken you that is not common to man. God is faithful, and he will not let you be tempted beyond your ability, but with the temptation he will also provide the way of escape, that you may be able to endure it.* I think of this and I thank God for His abounding love and forgiveness for my foolish heart. Another Casting Crowns song calls out to me, "East is from the West." It may not seem like it but I do listen to music other Christian music—it just seems to me that I relate to so many of the songs from Casting Crowns. Even thinking about the lyrics gives me chills: "You've cast my sin as far as the East is to the West and I stand before you now as though I've never sinned."

Letters from 2 Corinthians

I was muddling around wondering where to go next. I went through Philippians and Galatians because I seemed to find myself going back to them while I am in other scriptures, but God had other plans, he wanted me to stay in Corinth. So today my Spirit of the Prophecy read: "You are entering a time of advance when you can break through barriers that range from minor issues to significant and momentous change. Be alert and get ready to move forward as hindrances are removed and opportunities present themselves. Pressures that have weighed you down will suddenly lift, and you will experience a sense of release and freedom. Maximize this time of joy with thanksgiving and praise, says the Lord." 2 Corinthians 9:10-11: *Now may He who supplies seed to the sower, and bread for food, supply and multiply the seed you have sown and increase the fruits of your righteousness, while you are enriched in everything for all liberality, which causes thanksgiving through us to God.* I don't know when this lifting is suppose to occur but I sure wish it was yesterday, because I have been struggling daily for weeks now and I can't seem to move on. I feel like this heavy cloud is over me and as hard as I pray against it, it is not lifted. The only thing I can take from that is that there is something in it I need to see, because I know that God would not put me through this without a purpose.

It's strange but the troubled heart that beats through 2 Corinthians feels very close to what is going on inside of me right now. I feel it is time for me to break with those in my life who will not see or hear, because I am struggling with being patient. I am becoming more and more frustrated with the continual questioning, yet no movement. The more pressed I am, the more frustrated I feel right now, and I do not want to be in a situation that could push me beyond what I can handle in a Christ-like manner. I truly expect that one day my mouth will open up and yell out, "DAH! You are unhappy, unsatisfied, and empty in your life but you are not willing to change anything for the mere chance that you might find happiness beyond a bottom of a bottle, behind the wheel of a new car or larger boat, at the end of charge slip or hanging from the rafters of a bigger house." To have to sit and hear someone say, "If God is a forgiving God, we'll all go to heaven," like God has to pass our test by forgiving our sins, or "I live by the ten commandments, so I'm okay, right?" No. If the law was enough He wouldn't have sent Christ, would He? Last, but by all means not least, "In my world, I am God" absolutely makes me sick. I go out to relax and enjoy myself and it ends up turning in to a religious debate. My friends used to say I had a "Brylin Caretaker" sign on my back because I attracted all the nut cases, but I feel like I have a different sign on my back now, I just can't see to read it. I've come to expect questions from some of the people who have seen my journey unfold, but complete strangers come up and sit themselves next to me with the "soul" (pun intended) purpose of convincing me that their worldly kingdom is acceptable to God. I will listen but I will not let them off the hook: the truth is in the word not in the world, and if you want real answers you need to get into the word with a humble heart, as in check your ego at the first page. Not exactly Christ-like; I don't know why I'm feeling so impatient lately.

I know that God does not call us to surround ourselves with just other Christians. We are called to share our testimony with nonbelievers wherever we are. But right now I am feeling a little numb by it all. I feel somewhat distant and I am struggling with letting go of my old self. Do I let go of my old friends, my old works, my old interests, and be isolated altogether? It's not like there are a lot of people from church dying to hang out with a divorced woman! The whole scarlet letter "sin" drome lives; even in church I am a misfit. The funny thing is—that is somehow fitting! I should probably stop listening to Casting Crowns for a while: "If judgment looms under every steeple with lofty glances from lofty people who can't see past her scarlet letter and they've never even met her." There is way too much truth to their music. Maybe that is why God called me to minister where I am, because I feel just as comfortable walking into church sitting alone in a pew as I do walking alone into a bar and eating on a stool. I think I get it. In this moment, my burden lifted. God made me to be a fisher of men: it's not for me to reel them in it's for me to bait the hook with the word and cast it out into waiting waters. 2 Corinthians 4 just screamed at me today: *Therefore, since through God's mercy we have this ministry, we do not lose heart. Rather we have renounced secret and shameful ways, we do not use deception, nor do we distort the word of God. On the contrary, be setting for the truth plainly we commend ourselves to every man's conscience in the sight of God, and even if our gospel is veiled, it is veiled to those who are perishing.*

Paul goes on to say in 4:7, *We have this treasure in jars of clay to show that this all-surpassing power is from God and not from us. We are hard pressed on every side, but not crushed; perplexed, but not in despair, persecuted, but not abandoned, struck down but not destroyed.* In my Bible notes it says that the treasure Paul refers to is the incredible message of the gospel: God's good news of forgiveness and the promise of life forever. Yet, amazingly, God chose to enclose that treasure in people who are like "jars of clay." Clay jars are ordinary and highly breakable. That's what I feel like; once clay that was being molded and shaped in a million different ways. Finally shaped, I am being put into the fire. Will I make it through the rise in temperature or will I crack and crumble under the pressure? I can truly say today that, with the love of Christ, I am going to make it. Through the words of the gospel the process of strengthening has begun, but even as I am strengthened, my vulnerability will remain so that I may always remember the grace that saved me. I must never stray from the words that called me and the one who, through His acts, has made this sinner righteous: Christ. In 2 Corinthians 4:10, Paul continues to say, *We always carry around in our body the death of Jesus, so that the life of Jesus may also be revealed in our body. In 5:17 he says; therefore, if anyone is in Christ, he is a new creation; the old has gone, the new has come. That God was reconciling the world to himself in Christ, not counting men's sins against them. And he has committed to us the message of reconciliation. We are therefore Christ's ambassadors, as though God were making his appeal through us. 5:21, God made him who had no sin to be sin for us, so that in him we might become the righteousness of God.*

It's so amazing to feel Paul's struggle in this book; to see that human side of him revealed so honestly makes me feel like I can surely keep going. Pastor Tom went to 2 Corinthians 11 this week as he explained Paul's plea, "turn back to your groom be betrothed to Christ, don't chase after other husbands, turn from your sin and back to the treasure of Christ." Paul also warns not to be deceived as Eve was by the serpent, for by his cunning, your thoughts will be led astray from a sincere and pure devotion to Christ. That explains the constant battle in my head to stay focused on him and not things or thoughts of the world. The worship team sang "In Christ Alone" and I was taken back to the beginning of my journey in Ruth: this was the song they sang when I was playing Mary Magdalene in the resurrection play. That song encourages me so much to just keep on believing, keep on pouring my heart out to Him who hung on that cross writhing in pain that I might have faith in the love of God.

John MacArthur explains Paul's call to not be unequally yoked together with nonbelievers in 2 Corinthians 6:14 in this way: "Christians are not to be bound together with non-Christians in any spiritual enterprise or relationship that would be detrimental to the Christians testimony within the body of Christ. This was especially important for the Corinthians because of the threats from the false teachers and the surrounding pagan idolatry. But this command does not mean believers should end all associations with unbelievers; that would defy the purpose for which God saved believers and left them on earth." There's your sign, Kath! God has me right where He wants me; He has given me the strength and words to stand in Him, so the next time I am feeling weak I just need to read Paul's sufferings in 11:16 and I will ask, "Who is weak, I am not weak, and who is made to fall to the unjust, I am not indignant." Or as in 12:8, Paul wrote of his prayer for God to remove the thorn from his flesh and God said, *My Grace is sufficient for you, for my power is made perfect in weakness. Therefore,* Paul wrote, *I will boast all the more gladly about my weaknesses so that Christ's power may rest on me. That is why, for Christ sake, I delight in weaknesses, in insults, in hardships, in persecutions, in difficulties, for when I am weak. Then I am strong.*

All through Corinthians I kept hearing this song from Third Day, "Call My Name." This morning as I drove to work I asked God to let me hear that song, and two songs later it played. The lyrics say:

> It's been so long since you felt like you where loved, so what went wrong but do you know there's a place where you belong, here in my arms. When you feel like you're alone in your sadness and it seems like no one in this whole world cares and you want to get away from the madness You just call my name and I'll be there, The pain inside has erased your hope for love soon you will find I'll give you all that your heart could ever want and so much more.

It makes me cry that I ever questioned that He is alive!

Letters from Romans

The book of Martin Luther is, where people say he understood the phrase, "righteousness from God." This is where some say, that Paul explains the meaning of life. I have to admit that up until now I have found Paul challenging. I often felt that he saw women as subservient in his teachings, but I am questioning my perception. I wonder if I was reading his words through my own fear: the fear that I have of allowing any man to have authority over me is greater than I've even dared to fully feel or even begin to look at. It is hard for me to believe that there are men out there with integrity and grace who can be trusted to lead my life, my community, and my country with God's true righteousness. I do know that my thoughts on Paul have changed since Corinthians; the man I saw in Corinth, was not the man I had pictured in my mind. Maybe I am as guilty as the next person when it comes to drawing perceptions through the eyeglass of my own fear.

This weekend, I was shown a true picture of a man of integrity through a man I had my morning coffee with every Sunday before leaving for church. He is a man I never had the opportunity to meet but who taught me so much about politics and character by his dedication to his family, work and community. There are moments in everyone's life where they are shocked by the lost of someone who had a profound effect on how we viewed ourselves and those around us, and Tim Russert was truly that man for me. Some people dream of meeting celebrities like George Clooney, but I had dreams of being interviewed by Tim Russert. I have always been drawn to politics, and through Tim I received an education on truth and accountability. Just when I said I didn't believe in men of integrity, God up and takes one away without warning. There are times when I would like a debate over who goes next but I don't think my needs outweigh His plan. The thing that hurts the most is that Tim was the greatest ambassador for Buffalo and the Western New York area. Because of him, people around the world got a taste of the best Buffalo has to offer—and that is its people. In a world where people walk away from their roots when they achieve success, even flaunt their excess on "Total Excess" TV shows, he was a humble man who was grounded in his Catholic faith. In Romans 1:16 Paul says *"The righteous shall live by faith"*.

Maybe I am guilty of painting with too broad of a brush when I say I don't believe that outside of my dad and brother, there are men of integrity in the world. Maybe I need to stop living in fear and place my faith where it belongs—in Christ—and just live and love no matter what the cost. I realize now that all the things I have looked at as losses Christ has truly turned to gain, so who can say that one is guilty of loving the wrong people? I ask this of myself, "Don't all of God's people deserve to be loved as He created them?" The mistake is found in falling in love, not in loving; if we allow ourselves to blindly fall in love and it is not based on the true character of the person, it will die on the vine. My heart has a capacity to love that is endless; I am never happier than when I can hug someone and make them feel loved in that moment. When I can turn anger to calmness—through kindness or laughter, I am cultivating the things that Christ has planted within me. "Character is defined by moral strength and integrity," I wrote in the script for the children's show. Maybe what I need to do is define *love* and *falling in love* so that I can discern the difference in them as well. This was not how I had planned to start out Romans but I am ever mindful that God speaks through His word, and as He lifted me from my struggle through Corinth, I am excited to imagine where He will take me to in Rome. I guess I didn't really need to get my passport after all because in the word I find myself traveling through time and distance without leaving my home.

As I finally broke through my deep struggle in Corinth, I had received my Spirit of the Prophecy which said: "Be aware that the enemy will do his utmost to get you to succumb to discouragement and defeat, but I say to you, rise up! This is a demonic attack and is meant to demoralize you. You are not destined to live under the rule of oppression. You are dedicated to victory, for the enemy is under your feet. Again, rise up, overcome the works of the flesh, and war against these powers of darkness. I am with you to strengthen you for the battle, says the Lord." *Romans 16:17-20: Now I urge you, brethren, note those who cause divisions and offenses, contrary to the doctrine which you learned, and avoid them. For those who are such do not serve our Lord Jesus Christ, but their own belly, and by smooth words and flattering speech deceive the hearts of the simple. For your obedience has become known to all. Therefore I am glad on your behalf; but I want you to be wise in what is good, and simple concerning evil. And the God of peace will crush Satan under your feet shortly. The grace of our Lord Jesus Christ be with you.* When I read this and the darkness finally lifted I had to go to Romans.

So here I am, reenergized, refocused, and rejoicing in the faithfulness of our lord! It is time to dance through Rome! I can picture myself in the middle of the Roman Empire around 56 A.D., and much like today, there is a deep separation between the rich and the poor with a depleted middle class. You would see palaces side by side with the slums born out of the homes that once belonged to the middle class which have now been taken over by the poor and slaves. It was to this city that Paul, in his letter, unpacked God's righteousness imputed to us through faith alone, through Christ alone. As I read Paul's description of God's wrath on the unrighteous it sticks out to me that he repeatedly says, "God gave them up." He says the unrighteous suppress the truth; though God planted the truth in their heart, they chose not to honor Him or give thanks to Him, *so they are without excuse. So they gave up God, justifying themselves with their own wisdom and he in turn gave them up to their sin.* Romans 1:24: *God gave them up in the lust of their hearts to impurity, 1:26: God gave them up to dishonorable passions, 1:28: God gave them up to a debased, (to lower in character, degrade) mind to do what ought not to be done.* He finishes by saying, *Though they know God's decree that those who practice such things deserve to die, they not only do them but give approval to those who practice them.* It all reminds me of the worldly lies that we buy into everyday; to justify their own sin, the unrighteous pass it on to others as acceptable behavior.

I love Romans 2:3-4: *Do you suppose, O man—you who judge those who do such things and yet do them yourself—that you will escape the judgment of God? Or do you presume on the riches of his kindness and forbearance and patience, not knowing that God's kindness is meant to lead you to repentance.* Bam! There it is; thank you very much! The answer to my most frustrating rebuttal, "If God is a forgiving God, we will all go to heaven no matter what we do." No! Here's the deal: God, being the loving God that He is, will lead you to recognize your own sin, so that you will learn from it and turn from it. He will then forgive your sin through the acceptance of the final blood sacrifice of His Son as your savior. In the New International Version Bible it says in 2:5: *But because of your stubbornness and your unrepentant heart, you are storing up wrath against yourself for the day of God's wrath, when his righteous judgment will be revealed.* 2:7 goes further: *to those who by persistence in doing good seek glory, honor and immortality, he will give eternal life. But for those who are self-seeking and who reject the truth and follow evil, there will be wrath and anger.* Make no mistake there will be judgment for all and there will be accountability for all, for as Paul says in 3:23: *All have sinned and fall short of the glory of God, and are justified by his grace as a gift, through the redemption that is in Christ Jesus.* When I think of standing before God and giving an account of my sins, my behavior, my tongue, my heart, all that makes up my character, it makes me realize how important accountability is in all we do. I think about how hard it was to get the first children's show written and produced; I felt so overwhelmed at the idea that God had called me to this service. The responsibility to teach His little flock, knowing that I will have to stand before Him and give an account of every lesson was gut-wrenching. So daily I am as Abraham, putting my faith in God's promise, that through Christ I am made righteous. Romans 4:18 & 20-22: *In hope (Abraham) believed against hope. No distrust made him waver concerning the promise of God, but he grew strong in his faith as he gave glory to God, fully convinced that God was able to do what he had promised. That is why his faith was "counted to him as righteousness."*

When I got to Romans 5, I knew why I needed to be right there. Romans is just full of good stuff—what can I say? I think when people kept coming up and asking me about my faith, time and time again, I began to get into the mindset that they were questioning my faith and looking for the flaw to use for justification of their own journey. It made me start to feel defensive and what started out as joy began to turn to apprehension. I started to feel myself wanting to pull away and hide in a safe little "holy huddle" somewhere. I felt like I was losing touch with the Holy Spirit that I had come to rely on, but that time just helped me grow that much more, and eventually I found peace once more. In Romans 5 1-5: Paul says, *therefore, since we have been justified by faith, we have peace with God through our Lord Jesus Christ. Through him we have also obtained access by faith into this grace in which we stand, and we rejoice in hope of the glory of God. More than that we rejoice in our sufferings, knowing that suffering produces endurance, and endurance produces character, and character produces hope, and hope does not put us to shame, because God's love has been poured into our hearts through the Holy Spirit who has been given to us.* It's so funny that I felt so strongly about covering character in the children's show and here it is in Romans, not to mention the reflection on character I have been doing through the loss of Tim Russert. It amazes me how God calls us to question our own hearts when we are hurting. I couldn't understand why this man who I never met had such an impact on me, but when I saw the pictures of the rainbow that had shown on the final day of his service, I was once again reminded of God's promise. He showed me what a true man of faith looked like, how he walked, how he spoke, how he loved and I can rest in God's promise that one day I will have that interview with Tim because he will surely be in heaven.

A couple weeks ago my aunt passed away. It was my mother's first sibling to pass away and they did not get along at all their entire lives, but when it came down to it my aunt wanted my mother with her at her doctor's appointments up to the very end. My aunt had lived her life her way, but I had a feeling that there were some tradeoffs and some regrets. It seemed sad that so much time was lost over struggles which had long since passed and no longer mattered. As I sat there at the service, I felt numb listening to a pastor who had only met her at hospice a week before trying to make a connection to Christ in a life that didn't include faith. I thought it odd that a family that really never pursued or practiced any type of faith before needed comfort in something they denied. I could feel the uneasiness. Finally I had to say something, so I prayed quickly and spoke up. In that moment, what I needed to say was something real: that I felt blessed that my grandparents had four incredible women that inspired me in completely different ways. My aunt Alice taught me gentleness and kindness, Aunt Helen taught how to laugh at myself and at life, my mother taught me how to take charge and countless other things which were too much to mention, but my aunt Nonee, as we called her, taught me to "keep on, keeping on," no matter hard it got, believe that you will someday hit the jackpot; she inspired my entrepreneurial spirit. I count myself blessed that I had these women in my life for so long, and my only regret is that Aunt Nonee won't know her impact on my life.

These two funerals, though vastly different, made me realize now that my life is not about being comfortable and safe; it's about living every moment, not by doing for me or pleasing me, but leaving a carbon footprint of change through the love of Christ. I don't want to miss an opportunity to let people know that they matter not because of what they've done or who they are, but just because they are God's creation. When I think about all the kids that I've had in my life from CCD classes, 4-H, Pony Club, Equistar, to everyday at my store and now on the show, every one of them are or will be an adult, so when I look in the face of an adult I should be able to see the face of a child. How can I have anything but love in my heart? Children are where my heart lives and breathes, so I need to respond in a way that empowers from the word. What better way to raise a nation than with patience, gentleness, kindness, peace, love, joy, faithfulness and self-control? Through Christ, I have received the free gift of grace, as Romans 5:8 reads: *God show his love for us in that while we were still sinners, Christ died for us, we have now been justified by his blood and saved by him from the wrath of God.* 5:18 goes on, *therefore, as one trespass* (Adam) *led to condemnation for all men, so one act of righteousness* (Christ crucifixion) *leads to justification and life for all men,* so knowing His grace for me, how can I not give the same unconditional grace to all who come into my life? I will! No matter how uncomfortable it gets, I will turn to Him and He will comfort me through every valley and every turn until I see Him face to face. Only through Him will I find the comfort and safety that I have been searching for my whole life.

Paul goes on to explain the process of sanctification that produces righteousness in all who believe in Christ. Romans 7:6 reads: *But now we are released from the law, having died to that which held us captive so that we serve not under the old written code but in the new life of the Spirit.* In hearing the word, believing the word and following the word, a process is begun by which the law is written on our hearts—not to live *under* but to live *through* so that God's grace shines from within us. It is hard to capture all the gifts in Romans;

Paul lays out so much to inspire and teach, and his heart seems earnest. In the past I have struggled so much with his writings, yet now my heart seems much softer, as if the battle is over, and in peace I can see where my eyes were once blinded by the smoke of the battle. I hope that in my life, my words inspire, but I know that often words inflame, as I have many times closed my eyes too quickly, thinking that I was protecting myself from what was being thrown at me, when in fact if I had stood, eyes wide open, I could have seen more clearly. Past the smoke, past the debris to the quiet of the storm, standing with open arms, I may have learned so much more. As I conquer many things that held my heart's attention, and as my justification comes through Christ and not my own works or opinions that battle within me, regarding who He has called me to be seems to be changing. As Paul says in Romans 8:5-8: *For those who live according to the flesh set their minds on the things of the flesh, but those who live according to the Spirit set their minds on the things of the Spirit. To set the mind on the flesh is death, but to set the mind on the Spirit is life and peace. For the mind that is set on the flesh is hostile to God, for it does not submit to God's Law; indeed, it cannot. Those who are in the flesh cannot please God.* I think when I struggle with the word it is often my heart that is struggling with letting go of my own addictions, and once I can drop my defense and let God speak to me through his word, I can find peace.

I think we each have to be vigilant in watching for distortion of the truth within ourselves and others, even those who proclaim the gospel. We cannot chase the gospel for what we might receive outwardly but what we receive inwardly; but in the same way we cannot chase the gospel to validate our own self-righteousness. My conflict with Paul really came down to one word: submission. It wasn't whether women should wear this or that, it wasn't even the role of a woman within the Church; the one thing that really stung me was the concept of submitting to your husband. I think the reason it bothered me was that if I had submitted to the authority of the men in my life, I would have been a bankrupt, homeless, alcoholic without "a pot to piss in or a window to throw it out of," as my mother would say (in what we've come to call an Ethelism). My mother raised three strong, independent women; she herself was a strong, opinionated, hard-working woman with great drive and a rough but great heart. She feels responsible for the fact that all three of us girls haven't been able to find happiness in marriage, but I feel like God blessed me with the exact mother I needed to see me through living as a single mom—someone who would push me beyond what I thought I could be, not always believing in me, but being supportive anyway.

Sometimes it's challenging to listen to women who have had a "Pollyanna Life" (as my mom would say) try to explain Biblical Womanhood. I often wonder what Bible they have been reading. I was in my car listening to my favorite Christian station and they had a woman on air who was making an analogy using Proverbs 11:22, that brazen women are like "pigs: if you dress them up in pearls and designer clothes they are still pigs." Does it get more brazen than that? Talk about lost in translation. John MacArthur explains the same verse this way, "A nose ring was an ornament intended to beautify a woman in OT times. It was as out of place in a pig's nose as the lack of discretion was in a lovely lady." I was completely astonished that any woman would refer to women as pigs at all. Is it really necessary to degrade other woman to get your point across to women who have not had to walk the same walk? We have become a world that masks our prejudice in self-righteousness. The married stay—at—home woman seeks to slander the single professional. Why? Because of prejudice. The definition of prejudice is a "strong feeling for or against something formed before one knows the facts." We assume we know a person's intentions before we have even listened or sought the truth. We all started out naked in the Garden. Everyone's ideas seem to be slightly slanted to their interpretation and need; for us to cast stones at each other is not going to change anyone's heart. In the same way, I do not believe God has called me to cover my head, but that doesn't mean I would chastise a woman who did believe that this was appropriate for her. This all comes back to believing Christ died on the cross so that we would not be tied up in the law, because the law that was meant for good is the same law that divides us. Our own sins get tangled up when we try to put our need to control an issue that we fear out of ignorance into the scripture. It's so disappointing to hear shock jock comments on Christian radio; I guess it goes to show that Christ's call to love one another was not an easy request. Romans 12 says it best for me: *I appeal to you therefore, brothers, by the mercies of God, to present your bodies as a living sacrifice, holy and acceptable to God, which is your spiritual worship. Do not be conformed to this world, but be transformed by the renewal of your mind, that by testing you may discern what is the will of God, what is good and acceptable and perfect.* If God can transform my sinful heart through love, kindness, mercy and a gentle nudge, isn't that what we should also do? It's through God's transformation that the change is real and complete. I wrote in the show that God does not promise us a perfect life, but rather, that our journey will create perfection in us and that He will be right beside us even when the road is hard.

I think the word is evidence of God's love, commitment and patience for us; a book that was written over a period of 2000 years almost 2000 years ago is still the greatest guide for life. In every passage of Romans 12-14 Paul instills character in to each of us: *For by the grace given to me I say to everyone among you not to think of himself more highly that he ought to think, but to think with sober judgment, each according to the measure of faith that God has assigned. Love one another with brotherly affection. Outdo one another in showing honor. Do not be slothful in zeal be fervent in spirit, serve the Lord. Bless those who persecute you, Rejoice with those who rejoice, weep with those who weep. Do not be haughty, but associate with the lowly. Never be conceited. Repay no one evil for evil.* Romans 13: Submit to authorities; *let every person be subject to the governing authorities. For there is no authority except from God and those that exist have been instituted by God. Pay to all what is owed to them, taxes to whom taxes are owed, revenue to who revenue is owed, respect to whom respect is owed, honor to whom honor is owed.* I love how he brings it home in 13:9, the commandments: *You shall not commit adultery, you shall not murder, you shall not steal, you shall not covet and any other commandments are summed up in this word; you shall love your neighbor as yourself. Love does no wrong to a neighbor; therefore love is the fulfilling of the law."* Bam! There it is.

In 14, he goes on to encourage us not to pass judgment on another: *as for the one who is weak in faith, welcome him, but not to quarrel over opinions.* He goes on to say that one might believe one way and the other believe another way, for who are we to pass judgment on another's servant? *"It is before his own master that he stands or falls."* In 14:13 Paul says: *Therefore let us not pass judgment on one another any longer, but rather decide never to put a stumbling block or hindrance in the way of a brother.* Lately, part of my struggle is watching the young women around me who are struggling against so much: single parenthood, low paying jobs, abusive relationships, and no ability to see what is within them, being treated so harshly by people who have been blessed with so much and who should be able to be more compassionate. It sickens me and angers me, because I was that girl; the only difference is that I had the support and love of my parents.

I sit here and listen to self-proclaimed Christian conservatives touting their newest literary achievement that screams "right to life" and then they want to blame the downfall of society on single parents. How can you ask people to do the right thing and then crucify them when they do? It seems to me that the heart of Christ would tell us that this is the time to love. How can you, in your self-righteousness, endorse everything that contributes to a lifestyle of generational poverty and then expect the outcome to heal itself, and then on top of that, denounce the poor and hungry as a burden to society through the airwaves as you bail from all responsibility in your golden parachute? I don't believe that liberal handouts are the answer. I believe hand *ups* are attainable if we can get beyond ourselves and encourage responsible choices that empower people to make changes in their circumstances. Most importantly, I believe in feeding and nurturing our children so that they can rise to their own destiny; we are responsible to inspire, not oppress, and if we plant the seed, they can achieve.

I have truly had to lean on God's wisdom to correct this in a way that is from the Spirit and not from my own pain. In their arrogance they cannot see that being critical and degrading of anyone is an easy reaction but empowering someone is actually God's grace in action. We all have the tendency to think too highly of our own opinion, but as adults, Christian or non-Christian, beating down a broken person is inhuman. I love how Paul lays out the simplest of truths in 15:1: *We who are strong have an obligation to bear with the failings of the weak, and not to please ourselves. Let each of us please his neighbor for his good, to build him up.* Then he says; *through endurance and through the encouragement of the Scriptures we might have hope. May the God of endurance and encouragement grant you to live in such harmony with one another in accord with Christ Jesus.* What has hardened mankind's heart so much that we cannot even give each other hope?

Paul connects us to the prophecy in Isaiah with his words in Romans 15:20: *I will make it my ambition to preach the gospel, not where Christ has already been named, lest I build on someone else's foundation, but as it is written, Those who have never been told of him will see, and those who have never heard will understand,* which is in Isaiah 52:15. I don't know what happens to us that steals the spirit of a child from our souls and in its place seeds the spirit of death, but I know the ache in our hearts is one and the same. As we walk the earth wrapped in our own sin unable to see through the bindings that tighten every time we reach out only to be rejected, by another waging their own sinful battle, a spouse, a parent, a lover, a friend, a face across a counter, a desk, a bar, or even in a mirror, the only one who saves and brings us out from our graves is Christ! There's a song that was sung just before my lines as Mary Magdalene in the passion play called "In Christ Alone" and every time I hear it, I am overcome by the Holy Spirit and I never know if I will cry from the depths of my soul or be tickled from head to toe. In the final stanza it says:

> No guilt in life, no fear in death—This is the pow'r of Christ in me;
> From life's first cry to final breath, Jesus commands my destiny.
> No pow'r of hell, no scheme of man, Can ever pluck me from His hand;
> Till He returns or calls me home—Here in the pow'r of Christ I'll stand.

This is where we all stand: not one above the other, but all lowly before Him! Well, just As I was ready to wrap up Romans in Sunday service Pastor Dave spoke about Romans 7 and what he said brought more clarity to how our sin and the law became partners in crime. He explained that "sin is a law—an inescapable reality. It is everywhere and is the cause of all struggle. Sin is a war—God's plan vs. My plan, God's vs. My way, God's desire vs. My desire, God's Kingdom vs. My kingdom. Sin is a prison—we enslave ourselves to things that only give us a temporary fix but they don't bring true happiness. Sin turns all of us into addicts at sometimes. We need to be rescued from ourselves because our sin takes our heart captive." He went on to say "God will only ask us to do what will be good for us; even if it is uncomfortable for a time, so it will lead us to true freedom from our sin." I realized then that what I had been learning over the last year and half was to be able to say no, to discern the intent of others instead of being flattered or feeling obligated to bend to another's advance, and most importantly, to abstain from being intimate with someone until it is God's time. Amen.

Letters from Galatians

The children's show is now airing; who could have imagined that after all these years, all the hurdles, we would be running for the finish line! Just today I had a woman come in with her daughter who stated that she had watched the show and never knew we were here. After many complements on the show and the store, her daughter looked up at me and said, "Your store is beautiful" and that moment made all the difference in world to me. When I looked in her eyes I saw her future in what I am struggling to do, to change what is and to prepare for what will be. They say God sends angels when we least expect them and need them the most, and she was mine; her little light made me shine. I realized that I wanted my life to truly be a life of integrity that would reflect the love of Christ.

My Spirit of the Prophecy read: "The past has come up before your face as flashbacks of where you have been, what you have done, how you have failed, and how others have failed you. This is a ploy of the enemy to overwhelm you with sadness and grief in order to obliterate your joy, and it is a distraction from my will and purposes for your life, says the Lord. Use this time to forgive and release the past so that you can be free to manifest and express the fruit of My Spirit." *Galatians 5:19-25: Now the works of the flesh are evident, which are: adultery, fornication, uncleanness, lewdness, idolatry, sorcery, hatred, contentions, jealousies, outbursts of wrath, selfish ambitions, dissensions, heresies, envy, murders, drunkenness, revelries, and the like; of which I tell you beforehand, just as I also told you in time past, that those who practice such things will not inherit the kingdom of God. But the fruit of the Spirit is love, joy, peace, longsuffering, kindness, goodness, faithfulness, gentleness, self-control. Against such there is no law. And those who are Christ's have crucified the flesh with its passions and desires. If we live in the Spirit, let us also walk in the Spirit.*

Looking back on the beginning of my journal to this point, I am reminded of the Third Day song "Mountain of God" which says:

Even though the journeys long and I know the road is hard.
Well, the one who's gone before me will help me carry on.
After all that I've been through now I realize the truth that I must
go through the valley to stand upon the mountain of God.

I feel like I have been lifted from my pain, shame and guilt to a place of peace and extraordinary love. Someone recently asked me what my expectations were from a guy in a relationship. My answer was this, I expect that "we" would have respect for one and other, that we would respond to one and other, and not react, that we would hold Christ's definition of love (1 Corinthians 13:3) as our standard for one another. I say this as "we" because I would not expect anything from the man in my life that I was not able to expect of myself. I believe it is God's covenant to us that we have a loving partnership with one person; I think it is sometimes hard to wait for the right partner, so we make a lot of wrong turns, but I have faith that if it is God's will, we will all find the road that leads to someone who truly loves and honors us. For the first time I realized that I now know how to love someone. I don't know that I ever got it before; in the past my pride looked at the word "submit" and saw fear, but now I see that if you can't trust the person you are with to be able to submit your whole heart, your whole mind and your whole body to the relationship, you shouldn't be with that person. You can't test the waters, holding back enough that you can walk away and still have your pride. It's about laying down your pride for that person in the same way we do for our relationship with God.

The cool thing is that right after that God provided someone for me to test my new understanding of love on. This new road ahead of me will be focused first on Him and us next. Where once my heart was completely silent, it now beats again. It is so funny how the enemy can work in your mind to make you doubt the truth in God or to accept that maybe God isn't listening to our pain because his plan is different than yours. But the truth is that without a doubt that he is always listening and God is sovereign in all things. He knows when the time is right and when the transformation is complete. All the things that I thought were no longer possible in my life I can see in "the new guy." The one thing that I always held onto was that through my bad decision I had lost my opportunity to have a relationship with someone who really knew me, knew my struggles, and shared my memories, the one who, twenty years from now, I could sit across the table from and laugh with over all the silly things we once thought were so devastating, to think back on all the kid's first triumphs and tragedies. I guess I always looked at long, enduring relationships as a journal of a life well-lived, as in the movie "The Notebook." I've always wondered if at the end of my road there would be that one person who shared my journey. Through this process, God showed me that more importantly than the memories of a life well-lived is a life lived through Christ. Life isn't about looking back;

it's about looking forward to an eternal life. In Galatians 6:7-9, Paul says: *do not be deceived: God is not mocked, for whatever one sows, that will he also reap. For the one who sows to his own flesh will from the flesh reap corruption, but the one who sows to the Spirit will from the Spirit reap eternal life. And let us not grow weary of doing good, for in due season we will reap, if we do not give up.* In building this new relationship on God's solid rock, I will sow to the Spirit not my flesh, and He will be my unshakable ground.

It's funny when your child reminds you of God's promise in our life. When I told my daughter about New Guy, I told her how I had known him for almost thirty years, and that he had a four year old daughter. I asked if that made her feel uncomfortable seeing as she has a five year old son. She remarked, "Not at all! Hey, I guess God was listening to you after all. You always said that your biggest regret is not being able to have someone to share your memories of Talan and I growing up—well, now you can have that with New Guy's daughter and Max." Even at 28 years of age, your child always has a knack for seeing right to your heart. I had to laugh because I didn't even recognize the gift right in front of me. New Guy has not only known me for most of my life, he knows the loss of a dream but the beauty in the blessing, the struggle of raising a child on your own, the craziness of juggling a home and work, but, most importantly, we can share in both his daughter's and my grandson's triumphs and tragedies. Who says God doesn't know what He's doing?

In church this week, Pastor Tom spoke about our storms in life and that we should not be defined by them. He broke down Psalm 77 in this way: what was the presenting problem? God doesn't seem to be listening as we cry out. The underlying issue: we know the Lord of our past but are fearful that God has had a change of heart towards us. The essential correction: our resolve is set on the truth, remembering the God of our past is still the God of our future and we will trust him. Surprising conclusion: the glory of the Gospel is that we must not define our God by our circumstance, as His way is not ours. He knows exactly what He is doing as His thoughts are higher than ours. God led His people through the seas yet His footprints were unseen.

I just sat there in awe that he just laid out the storm I had been through. I stood on my belief that God does know my heart, He does know my burden and in His time, He will bring the love I had been looking for and so much more. It wasn't about me being obedient to God's calling me to be single. It was really about me having faith in Him beyond what was tangible to me—that He is the God of His Word; that He is all that the Bible says His is. Paul writes of God's covenant with Abraham in Galatians 3:8: *In you shall all the nations be blessed,* 3:14 *so that in Christ Jesus the blessing of Abraham might come to the Gentiles, so that we might receive the promised Spirit through faith,* 3:16 *For if the inheritance comes by the law, it no longer comes by promise; but God gave it to Abraham by a promise.* 3:24 *so then the law was our guardian until Christ came, in order that we might be justified by faith.* The enemy was challenging my faith, even at this level, and I was tempted to bow to the untruth, but I stood on God's promise through His word; I will believe in my big God! I believe that there is someone who is another part to the puzzle, who will fit into His picture for my life, and I will cast out any thoughts that make my God smaller than He is and makes my enemy larger than he is.

They sang a song in church that I fell in love with a few weeks ago, by Meredith Andrews, called "You're Not Alone," it begins:

> I searched for love when the night came and it closed in.
> I was alone but you found me, where I was hiding
> And now I'll never ever be the same
> It was the sweetest voice that called my name saying
> You're not alone for I am here
> Let me wipe away your every fear
> My love I've never left your side
> I've seen you through your darkest night and
> I'm the one who's loved you all of your life.

It's such a beautiful song and it reminded me that I can do this; I can open my heart up completely now and trust in God's timing, that He will guide me through it all, and most of all, no matter what happens I am loved first and foremost by Him, and He is the first love of my life.

Letters from Colossians

It's funny how sometimes God puts something right in front of us to make Himself known. The "New Guy" has opened my eyes to what I have been missing my whole life: we can't play it safe in love just like we can't choose who we fall in love with; that is God's will, and I can testify that anything short of God's will cannot compare on any level. For a brief moment on our first date we started down that road of looking back. I was reminded of a country song by Rascal Flatts that I used to listen to before I was saved. It has now been redone by a Christian music artist, Selah, and it is called "God Bless the Broken Road." I didn't care what his past was. I knew that God had forgiven me and laid my past to rest, so how could I judge someone else's past. I simply told him of the song and one particular verse that said, "The others who broke my heart they were just Northern Stars pointing me on my way into your loving arms." We didn't need to look back to move forward; I can't explain how freeing that felt. What I am experiencing with this new relationship is far more than I could have ever conceived of, and the funny thing is that he was right there all along and I never saw him. With all this I still had to fight the enemy, but I just knew that this was different; that this was exactly where I was meant to be. Yet the emotions that I began to experience were so foreign to me that I felt vulnerable. As I prayed for God's strength and wisdom I received my Spirit of the Prophecy, and it read: "That strange feeling of being disconnected is the first sign of separation from the past. I am indeed separating you from all that is behind before you can embrace that which is ahead. Refuse to allow these emotions to be disconcerting or to throw you into confusion. Stay steady and trust Me as I move you into new spiritual territory. You are in the early stages of being repositioned for greater productivity and fruitfulness, says the Lord." Colossians 1:10: *that you may walk worthy of the Lord, fully pleasing Him, being fruitful in every good work and increasing in the knowledge of God.* Feeling still like I was walking on water, unbalanced and unsure of my ability to just let go and give it my all,

I just said to myself, "I will stand on what has brought me balance, God's word. It has not failed me yet."

The next day "New Guy" called and shared the cutest story of his daughter as he made her her breakfast. It seems as though she likes her eggs sunny side up; she calls them "dippy eggs." I sat there for a moment and chills came over me as the Holy Spirit reminded me of two little ones who liked their eggs sunny side up and called them dippin' eggs and that they must be served with an order of *piecakes* not *pancakes*. That little unimportant memory let me know that God does know my heart and He was there even for the unimportant little memories. It was a moment when my past memories and "New Guy's" new memory came together and I could feel that much more connected to him. It was kind of like the opening of the children's show, "What was, what is, and what shall be," God's time is a continuum; from the beginning of the Bible to the end that calls us home, it is His entire plan, even the tiny little details. In Colossians 1:15-18 Paul really paints a picture of the length and depth of God's plan through Christ: *He is the image of the invisible God, the firstborn of all creation For by him all things were created, in heaven and on earth visible and invisible, whether thrones or dominions or rulers or authorities all things were created through him and for him. And he is before all things, and in him all things hold together. And he is the head of the body, the church, He is the beginning, the firstborn from the dead, that in everything he might be preeminent.* What a plan: set forth before the earth began, testified to over thousands of years by countless followers, and yet so hard for so many to believe.

In this week's service, Pastor Dave spoke of the change in our speech as Christ transforms our hearts. He said that our words are a mirror of our heart, and that we should always ask ourselves what the spiritual value of our words is. The Bible often makes reference to our speech and our ability to tear down or build people up by the words we chose. Pastor Dave spoke of how gossip and corrupt speech divides even the Body of Christ, that the Holy Spirit within us should make us feel repulsed by the utterance of it. It's so true; before Christ I felt that the power of my words came from anger, vulgarity or intimidation. As a woman I could stand toe to toe with any man in a battle of pride, but now I see so much more strength in speaking from the Spirit. Whereas before ears would hear, now they listen, but I can't tell you how hard the struggle of allowing Christ to make peace within me has been. Being raised with my mother directing "diligent debate Sundays" in between the Bills games makes it hard not to want to prove your point. There are still times daily where I slip and need that Spiritual nudge; at least now I recognize my sinful nature and can turn it over to Christ. That is why, as the sinner I am, I have come to accept my need to pray myself through the day.

Pastor Dave went on to lay out what the character of our speech should look like. I thought this was so great: "Only such as is good for building up," he referred to Colossians 4:6 which says, *Let your speech always be gracious, seasoned with salt, so that you may know how you ought to answer each person.* John MacArthur explains this, "Just as salt not only flavors, but prevents corruption, the Christian's speech should act not only as a blessing to others, but as a purifying influence within a decaying society of the world." Pastor Dave took it a step further to say, "Our speech should be used as fits the occasion; know when not to speak at all, be quick to hear slow and to speak. It is not always necessary to tell someone what's right, and that our speech may give grace to those who hear." He then mentioned Philippians 2:5: treat others with the same grace as Christ gave us. Our speech is a direct reflection of our character, so I guess I must ask myself if I want to be a Tim Russert, a man of true character or a shock jock, all rhetoric and no substance.

Letters from Philippians

I am struggling so hard with all the new emotions and feelings I am experiencing right now; it saddens me to think that I have missed out on so much by building such high walls around my heart. I think that when things happen slowly over time we don't recognize how high the stone has really reached. We feel comfortable and in control in the fortress we have built, deciding how far we are willing to reach outside and for how long we will expose ourselves to anyone who dares to try to enter. It's not really opening up to New Guy that bothers me so much as I notice that as I open myself up to him, I also become vulnerable in other ways. My conviction that we are all called to bring positive change to our communities, no matter what the cost to ourselves, my strength in my ability to persevere through attacks on my character; it all seems to be weakening. Or maybe God is changing the Spirit in which I stand in those times; maybe it's no longer necessary for me to take up the battle, but just stand firm in the truth. I honestly feel tired of struggling and fighting this faction or that circumstance; it's like the more I find peace, love and safety in Christ and the New Guy, I just want to throw down my weapons and run to them.

What is strange is that in my happiness I still feel an odd sense of loss for who I was, and more of a fear of who I am becoming rather than joy of a possible future that will no longer be based on how much I can do or stand within my own strength. I am disappointed at my inability at times to just put it all in God's hands and know that *His* will for me is greater than *my* will for me. Today my Spirit of the Prophecy read: "Do not be moved by fear or desperation. Rather be moved by the power of My Spirit, says the Lord. Be strong in the face of adverse circumstances, and refuse to take what others say or do as personal rejection. This is a time of change, which always produces feelings of being unsettled. This too shall pass, and you will once again discover that your God has provided the necessary foundation that gives stability, assurance, and equilibrium. Stay planted on the Rock of your salvation." *Psalms 62:6: He only is my rock and my salvation; He is my defense; I shall not be moved.*

The time has come for me to face the enemy in court; the case of slander that I had written about in Matthew has come to the point of no return. I had to sit and listen to the tapes of the radio show and it just tore me apart. I don't know why. It has been a year since it all happened; I had read the transcript, but I never really heard the voices and just hearing it myself just hurt to the core. It's crazy how life seems at times to be on such a pendulum, swinging from profound joy to devastating pain in a blink of an eye. Maybe my lack of joy in this new storm is the reason I am drawn to the book of Philippians, Paul's letter of joy. This letter mentions joy fifteen times at least twice in each chapter. I guess if Paul can write so fervently about joy while still imprisoned, I can find my joy again. Maybe in a way we both are imprisoned; all I can pray for is that even in this storm it will all be for His glory. Paul's passion flows so beautifully in the first chapter; his love and encouragement just speaks out to you. He puts it all on the line for Christ: in 1:19-20 Paul says: *Yes, and I will rejoice, for I know that through your prayers and the help of the Spirit of Jesus Christ this will turn out for my deliverance, as it is my eager expectation and hope that I will not be at all ashamed but that with full courage now as always Christ will be honored in my body, whether by life or by death.* What I really need to hear right now is 1:27-29: *Only let your manner of life be worthy of the gospel of Christ, so that whether I come and see you or am absent, I may hear of you that you are standing firm in one spirit with one mind striving side by side for the faith of the gospel, and not frightened in anything by our opponents. This is a clear sign to them of their destruction, but of your salvation, and that from God. For it has been granted to you that for the sake of Christ you should not only believe in him but also suffer for his sake.* This is exactly why the word has become my daily companion: where I once couldn't manage to read a chapter I now cannot put it down. It builds me up when I am weak, comforts me when I am broken, corrects me when I am sinful but most importantly it is like a love letter, always leaving you wanting more.

My Spirit of the Prophecy read: "Think about how it was when you walked in confident boldness to accomplish what you had been called to do. Then, realize that your courage has been undermined. Where you once walked in trust and certainty, you have succumbed to apprehension, self—depreciation, doubt and mistrust. This attack against you has been for the purpose of shutting you down so that you cannot fulfill your kingdom destiny. Rise up and take back what has been stolen and go forth again with a sense of purpose and power, says the Lord." *Proverbs 14:26: In the fear of the LORD there is strong confidence, and His children will have a place of refuge.* It still amazes me how these encouragements come at such perfect timing. My spirit was really being challenged; I am called by Christ to forgive and pray for those who come against me, and yet I am compelled to follow this lawsuit to the end, and I'm not sure why. My hope is that the station's delay will be installed and no one will have to suffer like this again. It's not like what was broadcast can be taken back; there will be those who will believe such trash no matter what works I do; what is done is done. Yet, the Holy Spirit keeps pushing forward within me that His righteousness in my life will be known, but I'm not sure what that means. The vulnerability I am feeling with such an open heart makes it hard to hold others accountable to the point of pain, but maybe it's not about me but about allowing others to see Christ's work in me. As always I know that my ability to understand His plan is so small, yet I still ponder where this is all going; why I have to continually fight lies and slander against my character, I may never know. Why is it that the more you do or give to a community the more they are compelled to try to paint you as some evil person just out for your own gain in some unfounded way? I hate the saying, "No good deed goes on punished," because it somehow justifies the evil that follows the good.

The ironic thing is that the works that I do are not my doing anyway, and so there really is nothing I can get from it. Before Christ came into my life, all the things I did to gain approval and acceptance from those who ridiculed me left me empty. Now I do all things for Him and I am full from my head to my toes, just like in Phil. 2: 1-4: *So if there is any encouragement in Christ, any comfort from love, any participation in the Spirit, any affection and sympathy, complete my joy by being of the same mind having the same love, being in full accord and of one mind, Do nothing from rivalry or conceit, but in humility count others more significant than yourselves. Let each of you look not only to his own interest, but also to the interest of others.* Paul goes on to speak of Christ's own humility as He made Himself nothing to the point at which He hung on a cross; from God, to servant, to sacrifice. I pray for that grace every day. As Paul warns in 3:2: *Look out for the dogs, look out for the evildoers, look out for those who mutilate the flesh, For we are the real circumcision, (the true people of God who have been cleansed of sin by God through Christ) who worship by the Spirit of God, and glory in Christ Jesus and put no confidence in the flesh.* It's like the more transformation that occurs within me, the more of a target I become to those who are enslaved to the world, because their hearts' desires are set on their own gain, their own idols, and their own power, so in their mind, mine must also be.

I thank God that He has opened my heart and my mind to the scripture making it my companion as I go on with my journey, because I know that I can turn to it at all times and find the answer I need waiting for me. In 4:6, Paul writes: *The Lord is at hand; do not be anxious about anything, but in everything by prayer and supplication, with thanksgiving let your request be made known to God. And the peace of God, which surpasses all understanding, will guard your hearts and your minds in Christ Jesus.* So in this time I will continue in faith and prayer that My God is with me and He will not let me fall. My Spirit of the Prophecy read: "Beloved, I have seen your trouble as you have come through a blazing fire of adversity. Yet, today I am imparting to you a new level of hope and faith that will carry you through the next leg of the journey before you. Feed on this mighty impartation. Soak in this conveyance, for I am transporting you to a higher position of confidence and trust. I have called you and empowered you to manage with skill the next phase of your existence, says the Lord." Philippians 4:13: *I can do all things through Christ who strengthens me.*

This weekend was my first test in my new relationship. It was a silly thing but had such meaning, because I could feel a genuine change in my heart that Christ has reshaped. I had planned dinner and as the time approached for New Guy to come over I hadn't heard from him, which is not like him, so I waited. I think we women have dinner issues bred in to us; I'm not sure why, but I started to feel hurt. I sat there wondering where this was coming from and I had to stop myself and ask God to reveal what was really in my heart. I was reminded of how Pastor Tom always talks about how our mouth speaks from the depth of our heart. He uses the reference that our hearts are like a cup of water being held in our hand, and that as we get bumped by things in life it is spilled out on to anything in its path. As I sat in prayer I could feel a softening of my heart, and a nudge that said, "Who have I made you to be?" It reminded me that this was my own pride sneaking up on me, my little world of self, and I needed to see beyond me to get to what was best for building us. The way I responded when he called gave me an opportunity to be a testimony of what Christ has done in my heart, that I can truly build a relationship on Christ-like principles and come away feeling more blessed, and much stronger in both my new relationship in my relationship with Christ. I realize that my past relationships can't even come close to what I am experiencing now. I don't think I ever knew the difference between loving a person and being in love with a person, but the difference is as great as Hershey's and Ghirardelli: both are sweet but one is heavenly. It reminds me of the song by Addison Road called "Hope Now:"

> Everything rides on hope now,
> Everything rides on faith somehow,
> When world has broken me down your love sets me free!

The Revelation of the Treasure

I knew it was time to open the book of Revelation and really let it speak to me. I had started it before and when would I reach Babylon I stopped; my heart wasn't ready, but I now feel strengthened by God's commitment to me, so that the time is now. It's funny—I wanted to go to Luke and look once more at Christ's parables but it didn't feel right as I proceeded. I think I felt like I wasn't being obedient, that my journey was, is and shall be His directive. What was even funnier was the CD by Third Day I have been pining for like 13 year old Beatles fan was called *Revelation*. Knowing how God works, I wasn't completely surprised when I went to church this week and our guest speaker Dr. Emmons announced that he was going to talk about the parable of the manager in Luke today and that tonight he would break down every chapter of the book of Revelation. It let me know that God knows my easily distracted heart, but again He asked me to follow him. So I went that night to hear Dr. Emmons with an open heart.

The first thing that grabbed my attention was Rev 1:4 where John addresses the seven churches: "Grace to you and peace from him who is and who was and who is coming." It is so similar to the opening of the kids show, what was, what is and what shall be. Then as Jesus spoke to the churches, I realized that I am each of the seven churches Christ described in Revelation; each dwells within me at any given time. Like Ephesus, I have done good works, endured much, tested false prophets, yet at times abandoned my first love, Christ. Like Smyrna I have suffered tribulation, poverty and slander. Like Pergamum, I have hung in the house of Satan, hanging onto my worldly idols, accepting sexual immorality. Like Thyatira, I have been taken in by the seduction of the Jezebels, those who would sell their soul for a moment of glory of this world. Like Sardis I have been dead to my core while giving the appearance of being alive in Christ. Like Philadelphia I have held on by a thread to the fact that Christ was, is and always will be my savior. Like Laodicea I have received gifts that never belonged to me, were never meant for my glory, and yet I dulled their shine claiming them as mine. To me, the seven churches represent the true heart of humanity; we are always caught in the middle and without Christ's saving grace we have no chance of not burning in Hell.

The connection to Luke 16 comes as a stark reminder of where my priorities must first be focused: being a true steward of God's gifts in me. I must allow all that I am and all that I have to reflect His face to all who look to me with needful hearts, pointing them to His Kingdom. Dr. Emmons stated that, "Kingdom stewards shrewdly maximize eternal investments." It is our responsibility to use all we have been given to bring God a greater return for his Kingdom. The realization that only 144,000 are sealed by God for his Kingdom, which leaves the rest of us who believe in the Great Multitude from every nation, not by anything we have done but only through the love of Christ. I love 7:15-17: *Therefore they are before the throne of God, and serve him day and night in his temple; and he who sits on the throne will shelter them with his presence. They shall hunger no more, neither thirst anymore; the sun shall not strike them nor any scorching heat. For the Lamb in the midst of the throne will be their shepherd and he will guide them to springs of living water, and God will wipe away every tear from their eyes.* How amazing that would be, how humbling, to be safe in the loving arms of the Father.

Yet as incredible as I can imagine that moment to be, it is just as devastating to know what is in store for all who have not broken through their pride to humble themselves as His servant or those who just never heard His call. With the breaking of the seven seals, so begins the great tribulation, the period that will once and for all break the pride of mankind. It makes me thankful that the tribulation I have experienced in my lifetime was enough to throw me to His feet. That my eyes did not need to see, my mind did not need reason, my heart needed only to ask, "Father, teach me of your Son that I may know your Love for me." That was the beginning of my brokenness, the beginning of my healing, and the end of myself. My prayer would be that all nations would know what I now know, that Christ is the beginning and the end. Through Him peace and love abide; for all children of the world to know that they are safe in their Father's arms would be the greatest blessing.

As I read through the description of the tribulation, I realize that my heart will not have the strength to bear what is to come. I am still carrying the pictures of the devastation of today's world: political deception, the immoral preying on the innocent, the spread of greed, envy and pride, the war against perceived evil brought on by false prophets, the slow death of nature at the hands of man, the loss of compassion for our neighbors whether next door or a world away. The battles rage here and now from tsunamis, hurricanes, terrorists, famine, genocide, rape and murder as Satan lives within the hearts of fools, and yet this is not even close to what is to come. So why are we not rising up in preparation? Why are so many believers still hiding beneath the church steeple when we should running an all out steeple chase across every country over every obstacle, spreading the Gospel in every way possible? What good is it to walk the walk, yet be hesitant to talk the talk? Why wouldn't we go all out for Christ, as He did for us? Yet many of us go to church to go through the ritual that was put upon us at birth with absolutely no heart for Christ or the Word. Only Christ can raise the dead, and all I can do is pray that the seeds that have been planted burst from their restricting pods, take root, and grow quickly as His time approaches. How amazing would it be to all stand unified in worship with the Great Multitudes?

This week at church, Pastor Tom spoke about not wasting our disappointments, that feeding our disappointments can lead to spiritual depression like Elijah suffered in 1 Kings 19. I can tell you there are days where I feel just like Elijah, like I keep swimming as hard as I can against this tide but still I am pulled under time and time again. Elijah says: "It is enough; now, O Lord, take away my life, for I am no better than my fathers." I can relate to that feeling of desperation as I read Revelation and see what is to come. At times, when I look around the world and to an election in a government that I have lost hope in, I feel abandoned. I look at the leadership around me knowing God has put them in this position for this time and knowing I am called to honor that, but I'm still disillusioned at it all. It's hard to know who to trust or believe in anymore and I think the amount of media we are exposed to every day has a lot to do with that. It brings discontentment, fear and discouragement to our table every night and it is the first thing we wake up to in the morning. I watch and listen in complete horror at times when those of us that should have a heart of a Christian pick political sides through the eyes of faith, knowing that the same democracy that this great country was founded on gives me the right every day to openly discuss my faith, to open doors to hearts that have not yet been captured by Christ. I love the beauty in the diversity of this country just as Christ loves His Church. I look at every change or misguided policy as an opportunity for me to become less of me and more of Him. Through His grace I am learning to bring about change not through legalism but through transformation. As I watch two good men go toe to toe for their agenda I am saddened that so many would go to the polls out of fear brought on by media attacks rather than in peace that God's leader will be brought forth for His plan rather than ours. They should feel at peace that they looked and listened to each man's hopes for this country, and they have chosen the leader they truly believe has the character that will lead us to a stable economy and world relations. Our faith should be in Christ, not a politician; our moral compass should be pointing to our own backyard, being His light, leading to His transforming grace to making real change, not in policy but in hearts. This political season I miss the non biased gift that Tim Russert had for listening to us, the voters, and asking real questions without speculation, without buying into party drama. I thank God that I have been tuned into the scripture and tune out the things that no longer feed my spirit, but create fear.

It seems fitting, that in our state of unrest, Pastor Tom broke down the development of spiritually rooted depression in this way: we experience disappointment due to our unrealistic expectations, which leads to discontentment brought on by our need to cling to our outside sources of happiness. But these idols never quench the heart, but rather lead to despair from dwelling on your discontentment. This then causes us to pull back from others, which leads to isolation and despondency, which makes us untrusting of others' support and input. It sounds like the same process in a breakdown between leaders, a marriage or any relationship we put our trust in. I heard a pastor one time describe the four horseman of a relationship apocalypse as Criticism, Defensiveness, Contempt and Stonewalling. When I look at the characteristics of all these destructive emotions, I feel it still comes back to pride. I think one of the things I learned throughout this whole journey is that our pride seems to always lead to sin and that sin leads to the destruction of our true happiness. The root of Satan is in our need to be happy and comfortable above others. We have become a nation that no longer respects sacrificing or giving; we give to others if there is a payback for us or as long as it is not any real sacrifice to our wants or needs, so when someone gives out of love or kindness we either have to attack their character or elevate them to five minutes on a morning show. According to the Gospel, loving and giving to our neighbor as well as those that we can reach out to should be an everyday occurrence that inspires others to do the same. It's kind of like that television commercial for insurance where it starts out as one small gesture that moves from one person to another, but I think too often our own prideful self-centeredness keeps us from doing so. I actually think the seven heads of the beast in Revelation are lust, gluttony, greed, sloth, wrath, envy and the worst of these is pride, because when you think about it isn't pride at the root of all these sins? Maybe that's where the expression, "reared its ugly head" came from.

Speaking of rearing its ugly head, just as I thought the storm had cleared, in rolled another front. It started with a confrontation from another professional woman regarding some volunteer grant writing I had done and was now administering. I am always amazed at how some people think that because they work in corporate management that they deserve to be treated with more respect than they are giving another. There comes a point at which even the Spirit of the Fruit needs to rise up and defend itself. I want to make a shirt that says; "Got Breast Not Lobotomy." It's bad enough when men talk down to you but when a woman does, it's somehow more offensive. If that wasn't enough persecution, I also had to have my deposition for my slander suit! I can't tell you how painful, humiliating and completely demoralizing it was to sit there and have to go through the degrading comments that were said knowing that people who have never met me will now have this immoral perception of me no matter what I do. I then found out it would only cost the radio station $4000 to install a delay system to protect innocent people from this pain. It saddens me that people choose to hurt the innocent rather than accept responsibility and hold themselves accountable. Radio Station Guy chose to go down this path of litigation over a $4000 business expense, all the while trying to justify himself with the first amendment. Did our forefathers really give us the right to slander one and other for our own gain? Was that truly their intent? A country founded on God has all but erased every trace of His teachings for sin and corruption. It's crazy to me; even now as the end of my journey nears, I don't think that I will ever understand the depth of man's pride and greed. One thing I do believe is that it will take Armageddon to break man's pride to truly be humbled before the Lord. Even my own, because the truth is that it was my pride that held on to my worldly works when God asked me to let go of all of it and follow him, so it was my disobedience that brought me to this anguish; it is not the fault of the pawns who follow blinded leaders, but my own, as I heard but didn't heed.

When I went to go home from the deposition, I was so broken I couldn't breathe; my feelings danced between anger, betrayal, and outright pain. It made me question my commitment to any community or organization that could twist my works in such an evil manner. Then I remembered the reason for Revelation, to cast out evil once and for all and to prepare for Christ. So my challenge was this: would I fall back into the arms of Satan and allow the perception that has held me captive my whole life to steal my soul or would I run to my Father's arms? Sitting in my car, I ran to my Father in worship with the Third Day song, "Revelation:"

> My life has led me down a road that's so uncertain,
> now I am left alone and
> I am broken trying to find my way, trying to find the faith that's gone.
> This time I know that you hold all the answers. I'm tired of losing
> hope and taking chances on roads that never seem to be the
> ones that bring me home. Give me a Revelation show me what to
> do cuz I been trying to find my way I haven't got a clue tell me
> should I stay here or do I need to move give me a revelation I've
> got nothing without you.

For the first time in my life I reached out to someone to hold me through my brokenness and it was New Guy. Instead of turning all of this inwardly on myself, questioning God's love for me or how I could come so far to only be facing the same haunting criticism, I allowed New Guy to come in and help me let go of it, and most of all to help me smile again. He was my rainbow after the storm and I am for the first time in my life convicted in my heart that he is God's promise to me. I know for certain that I have never felt with anyone else what I feel for New Guy, which strengthens my commitment and builds my trust and respect for him every day. His strength is allowing me to be a woman again, just as Christ prepared me for this moment by holding me in the palm of His hand, giving me the ability to let my guard down and allow a man to be the man in my life. New Guy is allowing me to open my heart and truly love for the first time. I guess Revelation is the one and only way through the past that leads us to our future. It calls out the divisions in our heart to make them holy again.

I was somewhat saddened by the thought that I had come to Revelation, because I thought it was too soon for this journey to be over when a friend, who I had not seen in months; (who I actually had only met fleetingly but was a fellow Christian) came back into town for one day and said to me, "You know Revelation is the end of time but it is also a new beginning," I think I get it now. I had to finally throw Satan's perception of me down the well of Revelation to stand firmly in God's righteousness over my own sin and put Babylon to death once and for all. My Spirit of the Prophecy said: "I speak to those who feel like you have to go back to the beginning and start over. But, the truth of the matter is that the ground that you have gained has not been lost. Do not try to go back, but rather move forward from where you are right now. Only leave behind those things that have brought regret and mourning. The best is yet to come, says the Lord. Come higher!" *Revelation 4:1: After these things I looked, and behold, a door standing open in heaven. And the first voice which I heard was like a trumpet speaking with me, saying, "Come up here, and I will show you things which must take place after this."*

While sitting in church asking God for wisdom in the road to come, I wrote a message to remind myself of what God has asked of me. God called me to serve Him not with a quarter of my life, not with half of my life but wholly. Doing works for those who are self-focused will never satisfy; it will be fraught with frustration and anxiety, poisoning my soul, leaving me tired, hungry and confused, for their goals are not mine and their ways are not mine. So it is up to me to follow Him who carries me, feeds me and comforts me. So here I stand on the banks of Lake Ontario with arms wide open, with the revelation that, just like Dorothy, the next time I go looking for my heart's desire, I won't look any farther than my own backyard, because if He isn't there I never really lost Him to begin with. Christ's ministry begins in our own backyard with us. With the Word as His map we must be mindful that our heart is often deceived by outside influences, but by making Christ the true desire of our heart, having faith that He is all He says He is, even when we cannot see, He will lead us over the rainbow to God's promise. The funny thing is that when I first met

New Guy it was in my own backyard! *Revelation 1:3: Blessed is the one who reads aloud the words of this prophecy, and blessed are those who hear, and who keep what is written in it for the time is near.* Father Bless all who read and understand.

It is done! Amen
But who do you say I am?

P.S. We now have an African American President, Barack Obama. What a great opportunity to rise to God's challenge and finally begin to heal our own hearts as a democratic nation, transformed by His Grace to be one nation under God, indivisible with liberty and justice for all. There is a song by a band called Great Big Sea that says, "This is my one small step, this is my walk on the moon." I pray that this is our one small step to establishing capitalism with accountability, responsibility, and showing our true ability to create stability for all of God's children not through handouts but hand ups. Yes we can!

Genesis

I didn't think I would be back here. I thought my journey was over with Revelation, but I guess my friend was right. Revelation is an ending but it is also a new beginning. The revelation is that I believe without a doubt that there is one God and His one son, Jesus Christ, sacrificed His life that I could live free from the guilt and shame of my sin. But sometimes to move forward you must go back, back to Genesis, the origin of my sin. I know without a doubt that we are called to purity in our walk, but for some reason that is a struggle for many who are called by God to follow Him. I recognize and whole heartedly repent of a sin that has haunted me my whole life. It has led me down paths that ended in heartbreak and inward anger and hatred, that led to complete numbness for many seasons. Yet even in the midst of painful regret there lies a yearning for love, a hope that one day I would find my Boaz. I thought that my Boaz was New Guy, but he was just same old guy in lamb's clothing. As I started to try and combine my walk with loving someone who had not started the same journey, worldliness crept in, and little by little, I gave in. As hard as I tried I could not keep myself from falling into the same pattern that my life has repeated and that truly, truly breaks me. I am reminded of God's promise in the Garden of Eden that Christ would conquer the Serpent. Gen 3: 15: *I will put enmity between you and the woman and between your offspring and her offspring He (Christ) shall bruise you head and you shall bruise his heel.*

It wasn't long before I found myself pulling away from fellowship, pulling away from church, and following New Guy, even to the point of doing another community event that he and I could work on together. Then something happened that stirred up my passion for Christ, and I found myself being ripped in two between two loves, Christ and New Guy. See, I knew I was being a hypocrite as long as I was in sexual sin with New Guy, but I didn't have the strength to change that. I knew no matter how I tried to set the boundaries; New Guy did not understand my burden. He had spent his life strong-arming God: he couldn't open up his heart to recognize God's work in his life even as he did everything to push Him aside. God had blessed him with a beautiful daughter even when he had lived a life of constant sin. He had a beautiful new home, a good job in a city whose biggest growth has been poverty, but he saw it all as his works, not God's. I also knew I wasn't the first woman to try to plant a seed in his heart so why would I think I would be the one to help him see that God had even more blessings for him? I was sacrificing my walk, praying he would seek for himself. What I should have seen for myself was that if I wanted a man who could lead me as a partner in life, in a Biblically-based relationship, New Guy was not going to be the guy. He wouldn't even open his heart enough to talk to me about my walk. He did not want to hear.

It's funny how people hide behind a religion when they don't even practice it. "I'm Catholic; my family's Catholic." Ok, but what is your faith in? A religion is not a blanket to hide under. When God calls you to seek the truth that is what you must have the strength to do. I told him, that I believe God calls all of us not by religion but by grace to seek a true relationship with Him. When we need correction in our lives—if we truly want to stop repeating the same mistakes over and over—we need to do something different. For me it was giving it over to God because I was and am powerless over my own sin. I was actually a practicing Catholic so I understood his steadfastness, but God called me to seek out the truth of His scripture and I had to be obedient to where He led me. I believe there are people across the world, in every religion, who God has saved by grace but there are many more who are spiritually dead, trying to hide in the security of a religious commitment that was made for them when they were children. I believe it is God's plan that all who are called by Him be scattered so that the truth is spread throughout all of His creation, that He has indeed risen and dwells within our hearts. He is the greatest farmer, planting seeds in every fertile land; no matter where or even how long it has sat dormant, God brings forth life.

As my struggles with New Guy began to grow, Grace Bible seemed to be going through a period of struggle in its ministry, changes to staff, outreach, music and just odd battles within the body that all seemed to distance me. But the truth is, going to church and returning to my sin was too haunting. Then out of a distant land came a young pastor (sounds like the beginning of a screen play). He started a Sunday night youth ministry he named LTO, Limited Time Only, in my own hometown. God put it on my heart that I needed to go and show support for this ministry, because I knew the kids of Wilson were struggling against so much. For a small town they seem to battle so many losses year after year; it's like spiritual warfare on a town. It was funny how God had pulled my niece and sister-in-law from the worship team at Grace to this new ministry, so I just had to go. From the moment I walked into this tiny church and tried to translate the Scottish accent of this young man, I knew that the Lord was there and that He was working hard. What I wasn't prepared for was how watching this ministry grow would affect my heart in the matter of my own sin. It was as if the Holy Spirit was determined to convict my heart of the truth of the relationship I was in with New Guy.

As weeks went on I received the greatest blessing God had ever given to me: my son started to attend LTO. He started out of curiosity, and it wasn't long before he raised his hand to come to Christ. He opened his heart from his walled-up Catholic upbringing to a new journey. God willing he will come to have a living relationship with God through Christ, as I do. What is sad is that many people have a misconception of being born again in Spirit. It is not a religion, it is simply the acceptance of Christ into your heart; it is for all who believe that God sent His Son to be a living sacrifice for our sins. It's not given out by good works, religion, churches, prayers, rites, sacraments or symbols you may carry. It is given by way of your heart and the Holy Spirit coming in and leaving a transforming imprint of Christ's love and mercy for us right on your heart. The Old Testament says in Ezekiel 36:26: *And I will give you a new heart, and a new spirit I will put within you. And I will remove the heart of stone from your flesh and give you a heart of flesh. And I will put my Spirit within you and cause you to walk in my laws and be careful to obey my rules.* In Jesus' words to Nicodemus in John 3:3-6: *Truly, truly, I say to you, unless one is born again he cannot see the kingdom of God.* Nicodemus replied: *How can a man be born when he is old? Can he enter a second time into his mother's womb and be born?* Jesus answers: *Truly, truly, I say to you unless one is born of water and the Spirit, he cannot enter the kingdom of God. That which is born of the flesh is flesh, and that which is born of the Spirit is spirit.* In my whole journey from religion to religion, I never got that until I asked for God to reveal His Son to me—not just the story but the man He was. I can't explain the change that happens. It's like a new life begins within you. It's like the Holy Spirit becomes your internal guide, like a GPS: Gods Personal Spirit! Unfortunately, just like having a GPS, sometimes we choose to ignore the directions because we think we know a short cut. I don't think you can ever be prepared for what the heart of Christ feels like; it changes how you perceive everything around you, including yourself and others.

When I think back on how I lived my life before my journey, I realize that I was so oblivious to the spiritual world around me. I was so busy just trying to get through life, providing for my children, trying to build a solid future for them, striving to change what I could to create opportunities for them stay here in Western New York. God was always in the back of my mind, but until my journey started I didn't recognize the reality of good versus evil or godliness versus sinfulness. I now know that whenever we move towards good there will be an equal opposite pull to move toward that which is evil. I believe that is what compounded my struggles with discerning where the Lord wanted me to be. Ultimately, I just couldn't be still and let my GPS direct me. I kept looking here and looking there trying read the signs but I was lost like Dorothy in the Wizard of Oz, following the yellow brick road that I thought would bring me happiness. In one moment, the business was having its best year: we were looking towards expanding again to a full play museum, the kids' show was off the ground and running, and I was in love with someone I trusted with every ounce of my heart. Then it all started to crumble like Sodom and Gomorrah.

In one year I went from such happiness to complete confusion, wondering why, after so much work, I was stumbling again. I now know the reason was that you can't have a relationship built on Christ and a relationship built on worldly desires. I see now that you can't have a foot on two separate foundations and remain strong when you are shaken. I fell so hard for New Guy and his little girl that I didn't recognize my own compromises as time went on. Little by little I was going down the same path that I had in the past, and even though the signs said slow down and check both ways before crossing, I didn't see the dead end sign at the end of the tunnel until it was too late. He slowly lured me down that path with a false sense of security that came from his badge little did I know what was really hidden behind it.

Financially, we took a big hit at the store and I took a big hit to my portfolio, so all of the sudden the dreams we had of expanding to another location or adding on to the current location started to fade as we lost our bid for a building that I could just picture children running through. The politics frustrated me so much, and now we could barely meet the bills, so how could we expand? Yet something kept telling me to move forward. But how? So I kept moving forward even though we seemed to hit one hurdle after another. It was the slowest year we had had since we started up and the problem was complicated by having a high inventory based on the growth of the previous year. When we sold down the inventory and needed to restock, all of the banks we did business with started trying to double our interest or cut our line of credit; it was crazy. Here the government was giving thieves bailouts and they were turning around and trying to strong arm us like loan sharks. It was so frustrating and the fact that our birthday party and event bookings also dropped to next to nothing, drove me even crazier, because the truth is that the only reason I enjoy the store is because I can surround myself with kids.

If the financial stress wasn't enough, I had written two scripts for the show to tell the story of Moses, and when I was ready to put them to tape, my puppet troop fell apart. First, Moses lost his front tooth, then Noah had to move his whole practice to a new location, then Daniel the donkey had a heart attack, and Mary the lamb got a contagious disease and couldn't do anything for weeks. Not to mention that the television station had to reschedule because all of a sudden their cameras weren't recording. So I was struggling through another slow Christmas season hoping to make up for the rest of the year. I had gotten used to having very plentiful budget for Christmas it had been awhile since I had had to stretch a dollar, but here it was. When I mentioned that Christmas was going to be tight this year to my son I loved his reply, "You know, Mom, I am so happy to be back here to spend Christmas with the family that that is good enough for me; I don't think Christmas should be about the presents but the people you have in your life, but don't tell Grandma that I said that," he said with a wink and a sly grin as he gave me a hug.

I kept asking myself, "why am I doing this store?" I could do anything with my education and experience but instead I am sitting in this poor city that never seems to be able to pull itself out of the depression it lives in. I found myself buying into the mantra I had listened to over the years from people who live here. It was not what I believed in my heart but as I struggled with all the challenges I had been through I began to weaken and my optimism slowly decayed to pessimism. I started to become one of the grumblers that I had always fought against. If that wasn't bad enough, New Guy broke up with me before Thanksgiving. I was dumb-founded; this was just out of nowhere. But the biggest mistake I made was letting New Guy come back without pushing him to open up about what was really going on and what his expectations were if we were going to make this work. I took his teary-eyed, "I'm going to lose the best thing that ever happened to me if I don't get my head out of my ass," as an apology and said we could move forward if he was committed to working towards making us a family. To which he said, "We can work it out; I love you, and my daughter loves you." Hmm.

From the start, I sat New Guy down and I was adamant that I was looking for a relationship that was based on biblical principles and that could move towards the commitment of marriage because I believe that when two people love each other they should create a family no matter what it looks like. I went on to say that I was not into casual sexual relationships and there are two things that I can't accept or over-come in a relationship the first is lying and the second is cheating. His response was, "I think we have the same goals and values." I took him at his word, but what I didn't wait for was the truth in his actions. It's not enough to say you think you have a certain character trait; you have to show who you are in your actions and your words.

My feelings were so conflicted. On one hand I had convinced myself that God had brought New Guy and I together, because I had honestly never had the feelings I had for him with anyone else, but over time I didn't see the same commitment growing in him; he seemed to actually pull back. I think my comfort came from the fact that I had known him throughout my life and it was like being with your best friend; you could laugh and play around and it seemed so easy in the beginning. Because New Guy and I had even traveled many of the same roads at different times, I thought maybe this was our time. What I didn't see was that my roads led me to Christ and the work that he had done in me to bring me to this point wasn't even started in New Guy. He was still holding his cards close to his heart as if he was in control of his world, methodically playing one card at a time, and he had no intention of revealing his hand or his true heart. He would always say enough, do just enough, or even buy enough to get by, but never invest in the future; there was always a void in his attachment. As time went on I started to see this as the Holy Spirit worked on me through the words of Genesis.

At Grace, Pastor Tom had started to go through the book of Genesis and as he got to Noah and the Ark, I remember sitting there behind my brother and thinking, "I feel like the Ark is sinking and part of me is going down with it." My brother and I had been struggling so much with what to do with the store; it was getting to the point where we were considering just closing it because the stress was getting so great. I can't explain, it but every time I would get to that point, the thought of not doing the show and not being able to minister through the store just wouldn't let me. Then as I listened I realized that my struggle is not with the economy or the city we are located in, it is with the fact that my sin over-shadowed His work. His work in me, the store, the show, and all of the things that He created—I pushed them aside to chase another dream, another desire, another longing. God had made a promise to Noah that because he was a righteous man that walked with God, he and his family would be saved from the judgment of sin: the flood. Noah saw the wrath of God, after which God sent a rainbow as a sign of His covenant with Noah that he would never again destroy the earth. In Genesis 9:20-27, Noah, the righteous man who was saved by God's grace, falls to drunkenness, leaving himself exposed for his son to see. His son told his other brothers and when Noah awoke to learn what his son had done to him, he cursed him in anger. But God's promise was kept by sending His Son, the salvation for all sin, through the line of Shem, Noah's other son. Noah's Ark, our store, is God's promise to us as a family, but if I can't walk in a way that glorifies Him, and if I strike out in frustration at others because I have lost control over my own sin, what was all His work for?

One night at LTO as I sat at a table with several adults and one of the younger girls, the young girl spoke of how hard it was to walk as a Christian in today's world because there aren't many single adult women to model yourself after, and that just tore me up inside. God put it on my heart that I was supposed to be that woman, and I was not just failing myself and Christ, but all those young women. I remember asking myself, "Who have you become" as I found myself lying prone on the floor in tears and begging God to forgive me and to fix what I had done. I didn't have the strength to leave, but I didn't know how to stay without New Guy opening up to me and Christ. I could no longer live in both worlds and I wouldn't choose living in sin with New Guy over Christ. I was praying so hard that God would open New Guy's heart; I knew all things were possible through Him, but that was not His plan. Shortly after this, it was

New Guy's birthday and as I prepared for it, I was completely unprepared for what was about to happen and what would soon be revealed to me.

Every year on Saint Patrick's Day I make a traditional Irish meal and invite friends and family over to pay tribute to our Irish heritage. So this year, because it was so close to New Guy's birthday I thought I would invite his mom and daughter, and we could celebrate his birthday, too. I got him something to open on his birthday and kept a little bit of bling to open at dinner with the family. I was so excited to surprise him; there seemed to be a distance growing between us and I needed to just love on him. Little did I know that he had no intention of coming to dinner; he had decided to chase another woman instead. What I found out too late was this was his M.O.: string one woman along until the hook is securely sunk in another. He called me the day of dinner to announce that he couldn't give me what I wanted. He never saw himself getting married. Hmm, doesn't sound like the same values and goals he professed to have before I agreed to date him. He went from, "Your faith inspires me to be a better person," to "I think your faith stopped our relationship from growing." I guess his timing shouldn't have shocked me as he never respected the number of times or the extent to which I would go to make him dinner. What I was about to learn was his stopping to have a beer was about the 17 year old servers as they explained to me what a creeper was. This was just the beginning of what I was soon to learn the man I had thought was generous and kind, who I could trust with everything, was in reality as deceptive and manipulative as the Serpent in the Garden.

Three times I asked him if there was someone else and, like Peter, he denied it three times. So for weeks he played on my emotions and love for him, texting me, "I love you, we miss you, Happy Easter, Happy Dingus Day," and stopping into the store, hugging me, kissing me, telling me he feels like he's losing his best friend, that no one has ever loved him like I have, and always promising to return my things when we could sit down and talk, after putting on a show of tears. He started to back off when I told him I went to church and Pastor Tom had spoken on the fall of Sodom because of sin, and how God had reached in to save Abraham's brother Lot and his family even though they had chosen to live in that sin against God's will. As it fell, Genesis 19:26 tells: *But, Lot's wife, behind him, looked back, and she became a pillar of salt.* God reached out and took me from my sin and I knew I was not to look back, so it was time to move on and get my things back before I left to visit a friend. His response was that I seemed in a hurry to get closure, "we can talk next week when you get back." I responded telling him there wasn't any more to talk about. He accused me of being in a relationship with Missed the Boat Guy, which was really funny considering what was about to unfold.

New Guy held on to my things until I found out the truth; he was pulling back because, he was moving his new "married" girlfriend and her two kids into his house. I knew that he had been working on this longer than the few weeks we had been apart. That was what hurt so deeply: to think he was telling me he loved me, lying with me and doing the same with her. The deceit didn't end there because I was soon to find out that our break up before this was for another woman. Now his actions turned all his words to lies as he explained "I wasn't looking for anything; we just met, I can't explain it. But I wasn't the cause of the divorce; I didn't want that burden." All the things I respected in him turned to salt. The fact that he lied, cheated, coveted another man's wife, and committed adultery, all in the eyes of innocent children made me sick. He actually had his daughter at my house for the weekend and two weeks later he was introducing her to her new family complete with dog. Society's lack of respect for the commitment's that are being broken for our own pleasure and happiness is what hurts our children every day. It is so ironic that what made him angry with me was that I wouldn't live with him without a commitment because I respected the feelings of his daughter. I didn't want to risk her getting hurt or teaching her something that I know now is morally wrong for children to be exposed to. How do you teach from a position of sin? What do you say one day when they come home and say, "I just met this guy and I want to move in with him?" What do you say, "Well, your immediate happiness is the most important thing."

But it wasn't to end there; as weeks went on more people came to me with more revelations of New Guy's character that just stunned me. He was so caught up in his own sin that he couldn't see the affect on his reputation; he thought people gossiped about him because he was 45 and unmarried. He couldn't see that it was the lack of character he showed in his decisions and behavior. It drew a comparison between the sins of Noah and Lot for me. When God pulled Lot out of his sin, his sin continued through deceit and drunkenness leading to incest with his daughters. Yet when Abraham struggled with his sin and temptation to not trust that God was in control and would protect him, leading him to repeatedly hide his marriage to Sara, God was faithful. One brother continued his life in sin and one fell upon the Lord's mercy. For Abraham, God's promise was fulfilled when He sent Abraham his son Isaac and when God tested Abraham's faith. This time, he was obedient and God faithfully stepped in and provided a substitute sacrifice for Isaac, a lamb. Even though I failed, I can find peace in Christ, my savior and lamb. Even when we are faithless, God is faithful! So my hope is that I can become like Abraham and turn from my sin and fall on God's mercy.

That saddest thing (and the thing that still haunts me) is that I realized that after all of the work that Christ had done to prepare my heart to love again, I had given it completely to someone who had a heart of stone. This man had so little respect for what I gave and did for him personally, that when it came down to it, his reason for our break up was that I didn't pick up the check enough. He had absolutely no empathy for the pain that he caused with his endless lies. But what truly, truly broke my heart was not that New Guy was out of my life, but that I let temptation win. I felt blessed that God would reach in once more and save me as soon as I recognized my sin and turned it over to Him, but it was that I had failed Christ in my walk, that, truly just broke me to my core. I kept asking myself, "Why do I do this over and over again?" That is until I woke up one Sunday morning and decided to go to a church that I had never been to before. It was a long drive, so I had put off going up and checking it out. But this morning I knew I had to go, so I told my son to see if his friend was still going up there and we decided that we would head up there and check it out. This was a large church and was somewhat intimidating but when I got in my seat and the service started I was captivated.

The pastor spoke of how the enemy uses our misplaced longings to lure us into our sin. So, in effect the enemy takes our legitimate longings for love, wealth, happiness, whatever it is that starts out innocent enough but then turns to sin through pride, greed or lust, therefore turning them to illegitimate longings. I knew then that, once again, my longing for love was used against me. Pastor Jerry said that we need to put our longings in the right place so that they do not become Satan's weapons against us but rather our weapon against him. He went back to Genesis 3, The Fall in the Garden and quoted 3:6: *so when the woman saw that the tree was good for food, and that it was a delight to the eyes, and that the tree was to be desired to make one wise, she took of its fruit and ate.* Satan had convinced her that the God who full-fills all longings was not enough, that he was holding back the best of what was out there and was not hearing the desires of her heart, so she chose to go against God's will and full-fill her desires by her own hand. She picked the fruit and ate of it and that was exactly what I had done. The man I thought was God's promise was Satan's son. God, it makes me cry as I sit here. It reminds me so much of a song I just love called, "I'll be by your side," by Tenth Avenue North:

> Why are you looking for love, why are you searching as if I'm not enough
> to where will you go child to where will you run,
> cause I'll be by your side where ever you fall,
> dead of night or whenever you call . . . my hands are holding you.

He is holding us, and that's what you see all throughout the testimonies of God's chosen leaders in Genesis. Even in our failure, God loves His people with a love that bears all things, believes all things, hopes all things and endures all things. He loves with a love that never ends but points to God's Promise for our lives: that He is alive and He saves. After Pastor Jerry's service I was starting to feel strong again and ready to move on, and then I would fall back into pain and tears. I just couldn't seem to get New Guy out of my skin. So I once again got on my knees and asked God to break off whatever bind I had to New Guy because I was not doing it on my own. I was still so crushed and found myself going back down the roads of self-doubt and persecution.

The next day, more of New Guy's character was revealed to me and it just continued with every person I ran into. I felt so humiliated and embarrassed that I had let someone with so little moral fiber into my life, let alone my heart. His lies, deceit, and sexual promiscuity, not just with me but others before me, were a long and winding trail of broken hearts—same lies, different hearts. I listened to the hearts of women he had hurt, including the mother of his child, and I couldn't help but want to hold them like they were my own daughters. I was compelled to apologize to the woman I was apparently the other woman for, and I realized how heartbreaking it is to take on someone else's sin because you take on the pain they caused also. As I listened to her experience I realized that when I thought he was being so respectful and waiting for me, saying: "It's okay, it's all about you right now we'll have plenty of time for me," he was actually having sex with her. I said to myself: "This is the final nail!" I finally got it; I am not responsible for the decisions of a man who lives his life with no conscience or compassion. There wasn't anything I could have done to change what happened. I was no longer going to allow Satan to use his weapon against me. I actually stood and prayed that God would bind Satan's hands and cast him beneath the heel of Christ and keep me from his harm. I felt strong again, for a moment.

Then as the words of these women played in my head, "He'll keep texting you until he can get back in to have sex with you again," something started to change in my heart; there was a deep dark feeling that came over me, and I had had enough of being played by men. It felt like the old me again the hard hearted me, even though I could hear God yelling, "Vengeance is mine." And even though I knew that New Guy couldn't really be hurt, because, like the Tin Man in the Wizard of Oz, he had no heart. I refused to be pawn in his game I was going to play the player!

So I proceeded to play him; I knew his weaknesses and I started methodically playing on them just as he did mine, repeatedly texting at the same time every day our secret conversations. Now he was Pavlov's dog. It only took two days, before he called my bluff by showing up unannounced at my bedroom sliding glass door. As satisfying as it seemed, I knew I had to end it, but he continued texting, "good morning", "hello", "Call me", and when I didn't respond he would call on a restricted number, or show up at the store. As I sat and listened to more lies and justification for his behavior, I realized that being rude and nasty wasn't working, so I tried the "stroke ego" text: "My feelings are too strong for you, you made your choice, and you have to let me go." In my anger, I wanted to manipulate the manipulator, but my pride needed to prove that this wasn't about me that this was who he was. But the *Holy Spirit* asked, "Really?" I responded by saying a firm, "Yes! This is not about me or any of the other women—this is a heart issue and just like any deep-rooted, habitual sin it can only truly be healed by Christ." That's when I pushed the mute button on my GPS.

The reality of all of this was that my vindication was superficial, short-lived, and it opened a door for him to continue unsolicited contact as he would try to connect with me through my past struggles with Manic Guy's drinking and taking meds. He put on a tormented performance of how he had never had to deal with that before. So I responded bluntly: "I closed the door on crazy in my life, I don't need the drama anymore," as I thought to myself: "Time to close the door on this too." I was completely dumbfounded every time he would so callously share intimate details about this woman he cheated on me with. For a year and a half I couldn't get him to talk about anything that mattered to me and now he even plays the faith card, "I appreciate your opinion because it comes from a Christian background." I couldn't believe I started all this because I wanted one moment of control, and now I was asking *myself*, "Really?" I had to stop responding to him so I could finally say, "I am over it!" But honestly, it was day to day, week to week. I would pray for strength and then I would give in to the next text, there was something I couldn't break away from. Finally I told him I had a date with a man I had met a church, Gospel Guy, and he said; "Have a good time," but the day before my date he came into the store again. He completely broke my spirit and I went on my date so guarded I couldn't even be myself, I was a mess. The following Monday morning he called this time asking if he could come to the house, and I finally said, "No."

My Spirit of the Prophecy that day was: "Beware of the enemy's distractions as he tries to open doors of accusation and insult against you. These are not the only places where he will try to come in, so be sensitive to everything that comes your way that will detract or take away from the purity of your walk in the Spirit. Rise up against every demonic intrusion; resist, rebuke, and bind him. I have given you the authority to stop these attacks and to walk in liberty, says the Lord." Luke 10:19: *Behold, I give you the authority to trample on serpents and scorpions, and over all the power of the enemy, and nothing shall by any means hurt you.*

It's so funny how He uses others to inspire and protect us, even when we are less than we should be. I feel so blessed that I can see His work and correction in my life and that I can praise Him for always being there through the storms, even when I am responsible for some of the storm. I knew that God was trying to reinforce what Pastor Jerry said at LTO that same Sunday night as one of the young men spoke on Gen 3:6-7, and our choice of sin and the spiritual warfare that we must guard against, just in case I didn't get it that morning. It was funny—my son and I both looked at each other with an eerie feeling about the connection between both sermons. Unfortunately, I didn't recognize my own sin sooner; I gave in to the pain and allowed New Guy to have power that he didn't deserve. I think part of me was so lost that I felt abandoned and I thought that all I had to fall back on was the old me. I can't explain this sick pain that seemed to take over my heart; it was so dark that I just wanted to die at times rather than feel it. Instead of putting on my armory of righteousness, I put on my old rages of seduction and control, but what I found is they didn't conquer, they didn't heal, and most of all they didn't forgive my shame.

What I learned through all of this is that the reason God calls us to walk in purity is to save ourselves from the pain and scars that are left every time we part from someone we thought we loved. It's like an untimely death; you are never prepared for it, and it doesn't matter if you are the one leaving or not. You may even believe that it is for the best, but the scar remains. God knows our suffering through His own Son's death, and He wants to save us from the pain and consequences of sex outside of marriage. In a day where the worldly values are invading every aspect of our lives, we need to arm ourselves with the word of God. I come back to Paul's writing in 1 Corinthians 13:4: *Love is patient and kind; love does not envy or boast it is not arrogant or rude. It does not insist on its own way; it is not irritable or resentful if does not rejoice at wrongdoing, but rejoices with the truth.* If I do not see these characteristics within the heart of man I love, I will not give my heart. It's not words that are important, its actions.

If I do not see a man walking in faith he can walk out my door, because a man without faith is self-reliant and will never be humble enough to love you through life. If a man cannot communicate his needs, he will be frustrated and resentful of yours. If a man has a bitter, unforgiving heart, he will never give you his whole heart. If a man is not patient enough to win my heart, why would I let him steal my body? I think this can be said of us women also. Our dating checklist should be a love promise to ourselves and God that we take as seriously as marriage. We should know what we need to do in ourselves to create a heart within us that can truly feed and sustain love, and what we would need from another person to grow that love. That should be our love promise: what we can promise to be to one another in a love relationship with God at the helm.

As I sat at home, trying to pray on God's will for me, I turned on the television and the satellite was out for all but the history channel, which had a show on the Acts of Paul and Thecla. Thecla was a follower of the Apostle Paul and she took Paul's call to celibacy to heart and carried that message to all the women. Of course, this did not go over well with the men. Twice Thecla was sentenced to death: once to be burned at the stake and the other time to be thrown to the lions. Both times God intervened; he opened up the heavens and it rained putting out the fire, and he called the female lions to protect Thecla, chasing the males away. I found it so sad that choosing celibacy and having the strength to not give in to the ways of the world could cause such persecution. But is it any different today? Those who choose to wait for marriage or maybe not have sex at all are looked upon as an oddity or naïve, when it is we who don't wait that should be the oddity because we are definitely the ones who are naïve. It is odd that we don't feel the need for true faith and trust in our partner today so we miss the beauty of all-out intimacy. It is naïve that we don't see the consequences of sex outside of marriage, the addictions, the pain, the children, the disease and the reality that if you give your body to someone who leaves, there's no payback, there's no return slip; it's gone! There's no "sorry" that can make it the way that God created it: the perfect gift. I can't even count all the hopes and dreams that I've lost because of my decisions, and now where my heart was once new again, ready to truly love again, there is a fresh scar that I feel ashamed to even ask God to heal. But I have faith that He will, because it was His mercy that revealed the true character of New Guy to me; without Him I was completely blind.

Even my son and daughter pointed out that we didn't really have the same values and goals in life. My son stopped me dead in my tracks when I said I thought we did; his response was, "Mom you would have never gone out and spent thousands on hobbies and toys, and not had separate beds for Val and I, and you did it on a third of what he makes. And you would've never let repairs on your house or your bathroom go unfinished for over a year—you would have fixed it yourself if you had to, so you didn't have the same priorities." My daughter chimed in, "Really think about it, Mom—it was always you who organized things for the kids to do, and when you did, did he really participate? It was always you who read to them and played with them—where was he? You were giving love to his daughter but how was he with Max? Max's Dad was in Iraq—do you think he ever thought about being there for Max? No, because he is all about himself. You were right in not staying at his place with his daughter there, and you made that decision out of love for her. You opened your heart, home and family up to him but not only didn't he reciprocate, he didn't even value it, because he wasn't getting what he wanted." If that didn't open my eyes to my blindness . . . The great blessing to come out of this is the strength of my relationship with my own children and that they see my sacrifices, even when I don't.

We went back to The Chapel this week and Pastor Jerry was speaking about the anti-Christ. I never looked at the anti-Christ from the point of view that the things that we put between us and Christ are the anti-Christ at work in our life. I guess I always looked at it as a power that goes against the teachings of Christ that will reveal itself at the end times. But maybe we build that power by allowing things, people, idols, addictions, to steal our hearts from Christ. We allow these things to enslave us, thereby building an army for the anti-Christ.

Genesis ends with the story of Joseph, who was sold, out of jealousy, by his brothers into slavery, but he kept his faith in God. God took favor on Joseph and brought him out of slavery to be the pharaoh's right—hand—man. In time, the same brothers who sold him came to Joseph for food. When they realized it was Joseph, and when they saw the power that he had, they fell down before him and begged him to forgive them. Genesis 50:19: But Joseph said to them, *Do not fear, for am I in the place of God? As for you, you meant evil against me, but God meant it for good, to bring it about that many people should be kept alive, as they are today.* Just as God promised Joseph that He would come to bring all of his people out of slavery, God sent Christ to guide us out of slavery to our sin. Pastor Jerry said, "The spirit of the Anti-Christ puts things before Christ and you can't really love someone until you can love Christ." That is true for both people—you both must love Christ first—it can't be just one of you.

I realized that the whole time I kept asking New Guy why he didn't fight for me instead of allowing another woman in to his heart Christ could have asked the same exact question of me. Why didn't I fight for my relationship with Christ? He fought so hard for me; even now He fights for my heart. If I imagined Christ standing in front of me as broken as I have been, asking, "Kathy, what happened, why didn't you fight for me? I thought we had this great romance; we used to walk and talk, and we had a great love for each other. Then you turned your back on me and walked out of my life. What did I do? What did he offer you that I haven't given you? I raised you up from ashes; I built your store and your show. Everything you asked for I gave you, and you left me for someone who never really loved you?" I can't explain how much that hurts; I traded my love and devotion for Christ for filthy rags, someone who couldn't even look me in the eyes and tell me the truth, who couldn't fight for me because he never loved me. Yet, I was still so torn and confused by my feelings of love that lingered for New Guy when he absolutely broke and humiliated me, but that is exactly what we do to Christ. He was beaten and hung on cross and we still fall into sin and put others before Him in our search for happiness. I am sure He is asking Himself, "Why do I still have love for this woman, after all that she has done, time and time again?" I am so thankful that Christ calls *us* to forgive those who sin against us seventy times seven times.

One night as I was getting ready to leave work, a woman came into the store and started telling me how she loved the painting I had done in the store and what a gift it was. She shared that she was a pastor's wife, and before I knew it, we were praying together for God to strengthen our ministry through the store. It was so strange because I had been going through so much frustration with the city and how or if we should or could stay; we had come to the realization that to stay we had to tie in to tourism with the museum expansion.

The economy hit downtown Lockport so hard that most all of the retail shops are now gone, and with the current mindset of shoppers being one-stop, with easy access parking, the hopes for bustling downtowns are dying. It would take a city wide commitment to establish and maintain an independent retail destination district; that connects the tourism district with an entertainment district, it's not creating a new vision it's getting back to what worked. I laugh when politicians and board members of economic development agencies say they have been in office for over twenty years, I want to yell, "Show me the money." I have watched the deterioration of all of the cities in Western New York for thirty years, all over greed and politics, and it all eats away at me. I truly believe the only way out of being in the highest taxed county, in the highest taxed state in a nation that continues to grow debt and overhead instead of business, is to go back to homegrown businesses. Just like Christ has been rebuilding me, we must build-up the businesses we have from within. It's hard to walk away from a place that I have so much love for. Lockport, like all of Western New York, holds so many childhood memories for me: climbing the Niagara Escarpment down to Dead Man's Cave, having my first kiss behind the veteran's rock in Outwater Park, and walking down Main Street holding my grandmother's hand as she did her Christmas shopping. So it truly was a blessing when this woman came in; it reminded me that God really knows all of the struggles within my heart. Gospel Guy, said; "Kathy, even Paul had to walk away and dust himself off from cities that would not hear." I keep hearing the Toby Mac song a "City on its Knees", and I pray one day that will be Lockport, but right now, just like me, my city seems lost.

That Sunday at church, Pastor Jerry spoke of how the absence of love for others, or hate for them, can lead us to more destructive behavior like Cain killing his brother Abel in Genesis. So I think we do have to love our brothers even when they fail us; it's not enough to just forgive, but I'm just not sure how. I know that with time my feelings of love for New Guy will fade and he will just be a sad memory of my looking to someone else to fill what only God can fill in me. My Spirit of the Prophecy said: "I want to speak to you face-to-face in vital spiritual connection. I want your full attention. I say this because many of My people talk at Me instead of with Me. Draw near so that you can see Me and know My intentions for you. Do not be afraid to come, for the way has been made for you to come boldly before My throne, says the Lord." *Genesis 32:30: And Jacob called the name of the place Peniel: "For I have seen God face to face, and my life is preserved."* My promise to God is that from now on He has my heart and He can do as He wills with it. I am no longer striving for loves that won't last; I am resting in God's Promise that He was, is and always will be enough. He delivered me from my slavery and this is my new beginning. Pastor Stephen started a series by Francis Chan with the kids at LTO called Crazy Love. I was so moved by it that I ran out to get the book. In it Pastor

Chan asks: "What would it look like if we had a crazy, relentless, all-powerful love for Christ?" I'm not sure what it will look like but I sure know where to find it: in the word. The next time I go looking for my heart's desire, I will ask this: knowing what my life was, what my life is, and my hopes of what shall be, is this God's will for my life? One thing I am sure of is that I can't wait for someone else to build a single parent support network, one that encourages and empowers them to make better life decisions. I need to step up and lay the foundation, because I know the struggles, I know the needs, and I know how to find the strength to endure.

P.S. I woke up this morning with the revelation that the reason I still feel love in my heart for New Guy is that, just like Christ has forgiven my sins and still loves and desires me, I need to forgive New Guy and to love him as God's creation. Not in a way that makes me weak or vulnerable, but in a way that makes both of us strong: by strong prayer, strong forgiveness, and strong love! Peace at Last! My Spirit of the Prophecy said: "This is a time of breakthrough for those who will leave the past behind and extend mercy to those who have used you, abused you or been unkind in any way. I am calling to you, My people, to forgive with a heart of generosity. If you hear My call and do as I ask, you will have peace with liberality; nothing held back. Let go of everything that holds you down, says the Lord." *Mark 11:25-26 : And whenever you stand praying, if you have anything against anyone, forgive him, that your Father in heaven may also forgive you your trespasses. But if you do not forgive, neither will your Father in heaven forgive your trespasses.* How amazing! So my new beginning starts now with letting go of my business in Lockport, letting go of my home on the lake, accepting, that New Guy was just a Serial Cheater Guy, and moving towards God's promise for my life. No matter what was, what is and what shall be God's promise lives in me. That promise is that true love, a God given love that sacrifices ones flesh for another's doesn't fail or fade it endures. So if it wasn't true love I never really lost what I didn't have to begin with.

My last song "Love Never Fails," by Brandon Heath:

Love will protect
Love always hopes
Love still believes when you don't

Over His Rainbow—Resources

The MacArthur Bible Commentary references:1 John 3:10-18, 2 Corinthians 6:14, Colossians 4:6. Publisher Thomas Nelson; 2005, Nashville, TN.

The Student Bible, NIV Version, Zondervan Bible Publishers, copyright 1986.

"Scripture taken from the HOLY BIBLE, NEW INTERNATIONAL VERSION. Copyright 1973,1978,1984 International Bible Society. Used by permission of Zondervan Bible Publisher's."

The Classic Thinline Edition, English Standard Version, ESV, copyright 2002 by Crossway Bibles, a publishing ministry of Good News Publishers.

"Scripture quotations are From the The Holy Bible, English Standard Version, copyright 2001 by Crossway Bibles, a publishing ministry of Good News Publishers, Used by permission, All rights reserved."

All Spirit of the Prophecy Devotionals by Marsha Burns. Faith Tabernacle of Kremmling P. O. Box 1148, Kremmling, Colorado 80459 *http://ft111.com/members*

Worship Music-Resources

The Beginning—I'm moving on-Rascal Flatts
Hebrews-I will Walk by Faith-Jeremy Camp
James-The Real Me-Natalie Grant
Hosea-Does Anybody Hear Her-Casting Crowns
Matthew-Today is the Day-Paul Baloche
Ephesians-Not Because of Who I Am-Casting Crowns
Isaiah-I will Praise you in this Storm-Casting Crowns
John-I can only Imagine-Mercy Me and I am Every Man-Casting Crowns
1 Corinthians-East is from the West-Casting Crowns
2Corinthians-Call My Name-Third Day
Romans-In Christ Alone-Natalie Grant
Galatians-Mountain of God—Third Day and You are not Alone-Meredith Andrews
Colossians-God Bless the Broken Road Rascal Flatts or Selah
Philippians-Hope Now-Addison Road
Revelation-Revelation-Third Day
Genesis-My Hands Are Holding You-Tenth Avenue North and City on our Knees-Toby Mac, Love Never Fails-Brandon Heath

My Love Promise

I promise to keep my heart open to whoever God might bring into my Life. Dispose of your superficial checklist:

_____

_____

I promise to seek characteristics in myself and my partner that glorify God. Memorize the honorable characteristics that you should have and look for:

_____

_____

I promise to stop running after those things that are not God's will for me. List behaviors that you are currently involved in that you need help in changing:

_____

_____

I promise to ask the right questions and expect answers that can be confirmed by actions, or friends. (Are you both who you say you are?)

Questions: What and who do you worship?
What are your spiritual beliefs? Do you attend church?
How many relationships have you had and how did they end?
What are your expectations from a partner?
What are your rules of engagement? How far do you go?
What constitutes commitment?
Where do respect and trust fall in building a relationship?
How do you communicate problems or difficulties?
What is your plan for the future and where is God in that plan?
What constitutes a family for you?
What does leading a family look like to you?
How do you want to shape your community?
Knowing who I was, who I am, and my hopes of what shall be, is this God's will for my life?

Let this remind you of your promise to yourself and God that you will look to Him first in all matters of your heart.